50 Years, 50 Bands, 50 Bucks

by Wayne Riker

ISBN: 13:978-1517704056 (Europe)
ISBN: 10:1517704057 (USA)

Editing, design, and layout: Liz Abbott.
Front cover photo: Steve Covault
Back cover upper photo: Jeff Perkell
Back cover lower photo: Dennis Andersen

Copyright © 2016 Wayne Riker
All rights reserved.

Introduction

My parents didn't play a musical instrument, nor did I, until I picked up my best friend's Stella acoustic guitar one day, in 1964, and said, "How do you get music out of this thing?" He showed me how to push down in the middle of the first fret on the bottom string, and I was immediately enamored by the sudden shift in pitch. By 1965, my friend had given up his pursuit of the guitar and switched to drums, whereby selling his guitar to me for $10, quite a sum back then for a 15-year-old with no real source of income.

After six months of playing by ear and eking out some basic riffs of the day on my own, I gave in and approached Dion Grody, a 13-year-old guitar *wunderkind* in my Bronx neighborhood for help. During the pre-Beatles era he was the kid who was learning guitar while the rest of us were playing stickball in the streets. I told him I just wanted to play lead guitar, as I wasn't able to successfully play a chord form. He laughed and said, "You have to be able to play notes and chords to play in a band." He sold me on that notion and by the following week he was hired as my guitar teacher at the cost of $1 an hour. We got seven lessons in during that summer of 1966, before my family and I moved across the Hudson River to New Jersey.

The next step was to add in an electric guitar because my fingers were straining to fret the half-inch distance from string to fret on my Stella. Luckily, the same friend who sold me that guitar also had an electric hanging around, so for $30 I became the proud owner of a 1965 Ibanez electric guitar, at the time a totally unknown and unproven Japanese company, making their debut in the U.S. that year.

For a solid year I explored the neck on my own with the guidance of the popular *Mel Bay* chord book, a useful dictionary of chord names and positions that I memorized, but had no clue about how to connect any of them. Fortunately, Grody had taught me a bunch of popular songs and turned me on to sheet music as well, in addition to showing me some basic blues scales and runs. As I memorized a bevy of songs, I worked tirelessly on strumming and keeping time the best I could.

By the summer of 1967 I felt ready to take that unknown leap onto a bandstand and cast my fate to the wind. Little did I know that an innocent hobby would turn into an unlikely profession, which triggered an eclectic musical whirlwind, culminating in the following memoirs: *50 Years, 50 Bands, 50 Bucks*.

—Wayne Riker

Wayne Riker

Band #1: The Xenomaniacs

Cafe Bizarre in Greenwich Village, 1967

The year 1967 was the Summer of Love, and New York City's Greenwich Village was bubbling over with a new breed of youth dressed in mod garb and long flowing hairstyles, initiating the transition from the beatnik to psychedelic era. In addition to the myriad live music venues, there was exciting hoops action at the infamous "Cage" basketball courts, rows of sketch artists lining the streets, and acoustic guitar jams at the southwest corner of Washington Square. One of the numerous club hangouts along West 3rd Street was the Cafe Bizarre, providing customers with high-energy bands seven nights a week, with daytime slots for poetry readings, bands, and aspiring folk singers; it was one of the few clubs in the West Village to have an accommodating dance floor and psychedelic lights. Many of the exotic drinks, all non-alcoholic, were embellished with a July 4th-type sparkler planted amid the crowning whipped cream toppings.

I approached the manager one night and asked if my band could play on Sundays in one of the open slots. She told me to come on down and play a set, and if people got up and danced, she'd hire me into the mix. So now I had to quickly solidify my first band. I had been practicing with Ronnie, a drummer from my Bronx neighborhood, and a bass player named Robert. Luckily, we had learned the obvious tunes of the day, including "Satisfaction," "Gloria," "House of the Rising Sun," and "Hey Joe," to name a few. We added in another

50 Years • 50 Bands • 50 Bucks

Wayne Riker in New York City during the early days

guitarist for the gig, who lived in Long Island, who frequented the club often. It was August and my first real time on a stage, my first chance in the fleeting days of that summer to experience the highs and lows of being in a band.

We called ourselves the Xenomaniacs, a wild name for a tame cover band, in contrast to some of the raw punk bands that rotated through there, with names like the Fugs, the Velvet Underground, and the Ultimate Spinach. Notable neighborhood residents would stop in for the ambiance and exotic drinks, including poet Allen Ginsberg and his sidekick Andy Warhol. I can still smell the draft at the club's entrance, emanating from the stench of the subway tracks below through the open grate above, and the alluring sight of the blue and red lights rotating from the stage to the dance floor. It was an intoxicating feeling of excitement to now be part of the whole oblivious and frenetic scene of playing music in the heyday of the psychedelic pop music scene.

Wayne Riker

Band #2: Polite Confusion

After a frustrating year of continuous guitar playing on two cheap guitars with warping necks, my spirits were rejuvenated after playing a girlfriend's comfortable nylon-string Goya guitar in the summer of 1969. Hence, I took a job driving a cab, while I was simultaneously completing 16 units a semester at college, eventually earning enough money to buy a decent electric guitar and amp. With renewed spirits, it was time to form a band. My friend, Dave, who had switched to drums after selling me his Stella guitar, was a logical choice, along with a friend he knew named Janusz, who was willing to switch from guitar to bass. Janusz had escaped from Poland, along with his mom, during the Iron Curtain days in the 1950s.

Polite Confusion: Wayne Riker (upper right), NYC. Photo: Joel Marks.

We found a basement room to rehearse in on 183rd Street and Andrews Avenue in the Bronx, a space that had little to no ventilation and leaky steam pipes, which created some ungodly hot temperatures, particularly in the dog days of summer. Since we were all living at home, the pressure of making a

Basement rehearsal room, Bronx, NYC

living by playing music was not nearly a reality, whereby affording us the luxury to play whatever we wanted, indulging ourselves in as much obscure material as possible, including tunes by Roland Kirk, Bloodwyn Pig, Frank Zappa, and John McLaughlin, in addition to some original instrumental ditties as well. However, when the opportunity arose to play at a few local bars, some of the more obvious artists, à la the Beatles, Jimi Hendrix, and Jethro Tull, seeped into our set list. Realizing that reality, it became paramount to add a strong lead singer, which became a revolving door of male and female vocalists over time.

April 1970. The Carol Inn, a bar I went to often on 181st St. and Amsterdam Avenue in the Washington Heights section of Manhattan, was a typical neighborhood bar frequented by a vast ethnic melting pot of characters, with many first-generation Irishmen lining the bar stools from early morning to the wee hours of the night. Noticing that there was a band playing there on weekends, I told the owner about my band. He agreed to have us play there the following weekend for the whopping sum of $20 for the entire band. Seeing as I was the one who booked the gig and Dave, the drummer was my partner in crime, we took the extra dollar when dividing $20 three ways, earning $7 for the three-set night. Oh, a couple of people got up to dance, but mostly we churned out tunes to the backs of patrons downing their mugs of beer while watching the Knicks game on the one minuscule television set, definitely a room that was better suited for a jukebox in favor of a live band.

January 1972. Finally, a steady gig. Yes, four consecutive weekends at the "lovely" Ferry Inn, a dismal-looking edifice sitting at the water's edge in the Hunt's Point section of the Bronx. On our first night there, we noticed the repetitive protocol at the front door, a relinquishing of all weapons before entering the premises. All knives and guns were collected and transported to a back room where many of the patrons had their own lockers, replete with their names on them, to store their weapons. There was a droopy fishnet curtain akin to what you see at a batting cage, draped around the stage, mainly to keep dancers from falling into the stage area, or perhaps throwing unwanted objects at helpless band members.

It was another typical beer joint gig, but we got to play loud and actually had some activity on the dance floor. However, on our fourth weekend there, the club owner had some bad news when he said, "Sorry, but I didn't make enough money this weekend to pay you," a line that I wouldn't be hearing for the first time in future gig exploits. After a couple of futile attempts to collect after our gig had ended, I gave up the pursuit. .

June 1972. Next up we were back to back Thursday nights at the Castle Keep on Tremont Avenue in the Bronx, alas, a club with actually some attractive decor, along with a small audience segment that actually listened to the music, albeit the roar of the elevated subway line, affectionately known as the EL, never seemed to be in tune with us. The only bump in the road was upon our arrival to set up, when we discovered another band was also there to play, better known in the business as a double booking. After some confusion and heated words between the two bands, we flipped a coin and won the toss to play that night. It was one of those rare gigs where some friends came out and you actually got applause for your efforts.

After three years of cutting my teeth on stage and practicing in the bowels of that Bronx tenement basement amid numerous personnel changes—surviving two holdups in my taxicab and eyeing the completion of a B.A. in English—I was at the common crossroads in life, known as "what next?"

Two life events were to follow that charted my musical course in a series of falling dominoes. The first was my English adviser in college, Dr. Unicio Violi, who recommended that I go forward with my band aspirations and forgo attending graduate school. He clearly recognized my immaturity as an academic prospect and gave me validation that I didn't receive from my parents. Second, the last gig with Polite Confusion was at Pace College in lower Manhattan on March 9, 1973. We had hired a woman singer, Ronnie, a couple of months earlier. She brought her friend Barbara to the gig, who later became my girlfriend. Both of them resided in the center of a tight-knit community of artists, musicians, and professionals, mainly based on the upper West Side of Manhattan. Upon graduation, I moved into that neighborhood and immersed myself in that scene, networking musical contacts that would initiate the many chain of events to follow.

Band #3: The Fandangos

Now on my own, in the summer of 1973, I was ready to meet the challenge of navigating a lifetime as a professional guitarist. My immediate strategy was to concurrently play gigs and teach guitar as a two-pronged approach to initiate income and to avoid a day job at all costs. As I began to assimilate into the inner circle of the Big Apple's music scene, five women, all symphony-employed musicians, had an available room to rent on West End Avenue and 79th Street, the perfect headquarters to begin my gig and teaching sojourn.

Word got out that there was a young guitarist looking for a band; within short time I got a call from Chris, a bass player who was a member of an R&B band called the Fandangos, which had a summer gig every weekend in East Hampton, Long Island, at a club called the East Boondocks. I found out I was replacing Elliott Randall in the band, fresh off his solo guitar work on Steely Dan's "Reeling in the Years," and who was heading out on tour with Sha Na Na.

Wayne Riker, Times Square loft, NYC, 1973.

The band was renting a crash pad to house all seven members, which included three women and four guys, along with myself. Using my best sports analogy, I was now moving up from AAA ball to the Major Leagues. At the

first rehearsal the drummer realized my raw potential but quickly spotted my inexperience, and didn't mince words when I started over-playing rhythm parts. I immediately got introduced to what "staying in the pocket" was all about. Then, I had to double a part with the trombonist, who showed little patience but tough love in syncing the part with me. Finally, Laura, a 31-year-old guitar veteran, called me out when I played my own fake Chuck Berry guitar intro. My solution for any and all my shortcomings was simple: take it as an exciting challenge and an opportunity to grow from it, whereby immediately correcting deficiencies in obsessive all day practicing.

It was a high-level musical unit with a great out-front soul singer named Carol and a dynamic trumpeter, Lauren, whose main gig was with the renowned all-female R&B group Isis. The set list was heavy Motown, along with Carole King and Aretha Franklin tunes, mixed in with some of the soul and blues standards of the day. The East Boondocks had a strange layout— the band played in a cordoned-off back room for people to dance or listen and an isolated front room with full bar and televisions. When the summer ended my confidence was high. I passed the first test of a pro gig and came away with confidence and excitement to move on to the next challenge. Most notably, the other musicians took notice of my rapid ability and discipline in learning whatever it took to fit the bill in their musical repertoire.

Wayne Riker

Band #4: Times Square

As luck would have it, in the fall of 1973, the trombone player in the Fandangos, Al Alpert, who doubled on bass guitar, had a lead on a unique living space in Times Square: an abandoned radio station that spanned the upper three floors of a six-story building at 117 W. 46th Street, only accessible by a freight elevator. A well-known mural artist, Al Loving, rented out the rooms to various folks in the arts. He was devoted to moving the arts scene from Greenwich Village to midtown. There were 19 guys living there, including artists, photographers, and actors, as well as musicians, along with a few women who rented space for art studios. A slumlord provided the space, so, as far as anyone knew, the building was abandoned. We affectionately dubbed it "the loft."

Times Square: Wayne Riker (far left)

The High School of Performing Arts was directly across the street, the same school that the TV show "Fame" was predicated on. Their music room was eye level to our bedrooms, so every morning we'd jam back and forth, six stories above the madding midtown Manhattan crowd bustling below. At nighttime we'd hold jam sessions as word got around about this cool musician's loft in Times Square. Local hotshot musicians traipsed in and out, including John Abercrombie, June Millington, George Wadenius, Michael Urbaniak, and Ron McClure, to name a few.

Unfortunately there was no heat and the cockroaches permeated the entire premises. I slept on an old mattress with a sleeping bag, waking up every morning with armies of cockroaches all over me, but it was the most exhila-

Catskill Mountains, New York, 1973

rating year of musical growth. In addition to myself and the bass player, Al, a drummer, Bo, who also resided at the loft, was available and eager to play with us. In the meantime Al had been contacted by a keyboard player from Brooklyn by the name of Marc, who was already in the loop to get immediate gigs. After a number of crash rehearsals, we were ready to roll and established Times Square as our default name in honor of the notorious neighborhood we resided in.

Our first series of gigs took place at the Italian resorts in the Catskills, set in pristine locales that were nestled in the rustic landscape amid the changing colors in the autumn of 1973. Suddenly, I was thrust into the big-league entertainment world, backing comedians and singers, wearing suits and tuxedos, while observing first hand from the veteran singer and keyboardist, Marc, the art of entertaining an audience while keeping them in the room with drinks flowing and patrons dancing.

I was thrown into immediate baptism by fire, having to learn, in short order, Latin rhythms, swing tune nuances, jazz standards, current pop tunes, and ethnic numbers, along with every obligatory occasion ditty from the "Anniversary Waltz" to "Auld Lang Syne." Often, Al would turn to me on stage and say, "If you don't know what to play, turn your volume off and use it as an ear training moment." Nothing like tough love to inspire me to show him up each following night with something new that I would learn that day in my obsessive drive for perfection and thirst for knowledge.

October 25, 1973. The gig at Il Dante's on Kings Highway in Brooklyn, a restaurant bar with tawdry décor, was my first experience playing behind a stripper for a few tunes preceding our dance set. Good thing the veteran guys in the band knew the appropriate tunes to play, from "Sweet Georgia Brown" to "The Stripper."

On another night there we got to open for the Platters, well, at least one of the zillion versions of that group. During the course of the night a black Cadillac pulled up to the front entrance. Two goons bolted out, entered the club, and proceeded to toss a targeted guy at the bar through the front glass window and onto the sidewalk.

November 1973. Playing a gig at the Lincoln Lounge in Staten Island, we were alternating with another band, one set on, one set off. The club owner didn't want us intermingling with his clientele during our off time, so we were shuttled off into a utility closet that barely fit the four of us, amid the dank smells of mops and disinfectants, trapped until we would be freed to play our next set.

These series of gigs set in motion a learning curve, over the course of four years, that was equal to studying at a musical conservatory. My band mates were kind enough to take me under their wing and tutor me in playing the nuances in many different musical styles. Through their ongoing tough love, they challenged me at every musical turn. I responded with tireless hours on my instrument, working out of books, transcribing solos, and playing along to albums of all styles in order to adequately keep up with each new musical challenge that confronted me on stage.

Band #5: Crazy Elephant

Crazy Elephant: Wayne Riker (far right)

Times Square added a female vocalist, suggested by our agent, Van Joyce, and suddenly we were the new touring band for Crazy Elephant, one of the many iconic one-hit wonders of the later 1960s. Many of our gigs happened along the Jersey Shore during its heyday in the early 1970s, from the crappiest dive bars to the top of the marquee billings at the more notable clubs. We were billed as "million dollar sellers, Crazy Elephant appearing tonight," often trumping other local acts, including an up-and-coming singer named Bruce Springsteen. Nothing like having a recognizable hit song to draw folks to your gig.

January 1974. We played a four-night gig at the Seabreeze Club at the naval base in Lakehurst, New Jersey, the historic site of the 1937 Hindenburg disaster. It. was my first gig at a military base, and a whole new experience, especially playing at the EM club, occupied by scores of young sailors ready to cut loose, sometimes heckling and often screaming out, "Play some Hendrix." Our keyboardist, Marc, got a speeding ticket on the last day there and was detained for the night.

January 21, 1974. Our one-night gig at the infamous Village Gate in

Greenwich Village was a personal thrill, a stage where I had seen many of my jazz heroes perform in previous years. The audience was filled with friends, past and present, from the colorful characters in the artist commune I was living in to Paul, my best friend in college, and my ex girlfriend, Carole, who had won her battle with encephalitis. Our gig was broadcast on WBAI in New York City, a radio station where my oldest brother, Don, had once hosted a Sunday afternoon jazz show.

Satellite Lounge, Cookstown, New Jersey, 1974

February 1974. During our gig at the Satellite Lounge in Cookstown, New Jersey, the owner, Carlo Rossi, never came out of a room in the back; nobody ever saw him, but he would send notes to his managers about what to tell the band, usually the obligatory "turn it down" memo. He was a stickler for bands playing too loud, once known to have fired his shotgun through one of Foghat's PA speakers and taken an axe to one of Anthrax's amplifiers when they wouldn't turn it down. The gig went from 9 p.m. to 5 a.m. with two bands alternating sets on two different stages. Since that gig I could now tell people, "Yeah, I had a 9 to 5 job once." Rossi must have made a deal with local officials, an offer "they couldn't refuse," to keep his lounge open until 5 a.m.

Change was in the air. Oh, no, here we go again: personnel changes, a familiar pattern that would become fortuitous for the present and the future.

Band #6: The Peppermint Rainbow

Wayne Riker, 1974

Marc and I survived the dissolution of Crazy Elephant, but before we knew it our agent persuaded us to become a touring group for another one-hit wonder outfit: the Peppermint Rainbow. Teamed with four inner city and groove-oriented Puerto Rican band mates, it was a far cry from the lily-white image of the original Peppermint Rainbow. Our agent suggested a video-taped demo over an audio demo tape for promotion. Back in 1974 that seemed like overkill and unnecessary, but looking back now he was way ahead of his time.

March and April 1974. The Jade Fountain, an inconspicuous Japanese restaurant, located just off the intersection of Route 4 and Route 17 in Paramus, New Jersey, was our first gig, a house gig back in that bygone era when playing six nights a week in the same room for extended weeks and months was the norm for many a club band. One great perk was enjoying a complimentary buffet every night before we played, a rare commodity for working musicians.

It was the height of the funk and disco era, so the challenges of some of our set list demanded a lot of work with tricky riffs and rhythms from such groups as Graham Central Station, the O'Jays, Average White Band, Tower of Power, and Stevie Wonder. Our bass player, Pete, was a slave driver and demanded perfection from me. Any note or chord, not mimicked exactly like the record, would have him incessantly barking at me on stage. It didn't help that he had a severe drinking problem and could occasionally be found sleeping under a table in a drunken stupor during our last set. Per usual, tough love from others just made me work harder; I was always excited to take on the challenge of gaining the other band mates' approval, anxious for redemption on each following night in an "I'll show you" frame of mind.

April 1974. In 1974, the drinking age was 18 in the state of New York. However, the club owner at the Good Life Bar in Lake Ronkonkoma, Long Island, where we had a one-week engagement, had a notice on the front door that read: "Must be 23 and above to enter." It was the first and last time I'd ever see that, but I guess it's legal for a bar owner to set a higher age limit for a drinking establishment.

May 1974. Back to the Jersey Shore and a cushy lounge gig at the Quarterdeck in Shipbottom, New Jersey. Lo and behold our bass player, Pete, didn't show up for one of our weekend gigs there. Marc and I covered the night as best we could with bass lines on our respective instruments. Luckily, it was a listening room; not many figured out the handicap we were under. Fortunately, part of my rigorous practice routine was learning walking bass lines on my guitar and it sure came in handy that night.

May 1974. The Swizzle Stick Lounge in Waterbury, Connecticut, would be one of a number of gigs playing in a club adjoined by a bowling alley. Due to the usual bumper-to-bumper traffic heading from midtown Manhattan to suburban Connecticut, we arrived 45 minutes late of our starting time. We called the club and told them we were on our way over from the nearby motel where we were staying. As we were scurrying to get changed and hustle over to load in and set up, our drummer Artie, a bit fried from his chronic cocaine habit, asked if he had time to take a bath. After our obvious negative retort to him, we still wound up starting an hour and a half late.

It turned out to be a good five-night gig with a packed club and full dance floor each night, aided by the good fortune of the bowling alley being soundproofed from the stage area.

May and June 1974. The gig at the Traveler's Hotel in Queens, adjacent to La Guardia Airport, would be my last gig in New York City. I played a week of the two-week engagement with pneumonia, barely able to make it through, but there are no sick days in show biz.

Two memorable moments occurred during that two-week engagement. As we were playing a tune on stage one night, Marc suddenly bolted away from his electric piano and stormed off the stage. His girlfriend was apparently being groped by a suave-looking guy at the bar. After a heated exchange he returned to finish the song. We later found out the guy was a pitcher for the Yankees.

The following night the club owner talked us into having his nephew sing a tune with us. He starts singing "Colour My World." A few measures in, we quickly realized that the lyrics were moving twice as fast as the chord changes; we were cracking up behind all the vocal chaos while trying to keep up with the transmuted version. Per usual, the audience had no idea about the musical train wreck.

Band #7: The Heartland Band

The Heartland Band, Wayne Riker (second from right), 1974

The offer from my brother, Walt, who was the drummer in a highly successful show/dance band in Kansas, was too tempting to pass up. Marc and I had been in three consecutive bands together, so he, too, decided to relocate to Kansas to join the Heartland Band. It was amazing that Marc's VW Squareback made it from the Big Apple to Lawrence, Kansas, with our worldly possessions weighing down the entire capacity of the car. I crashed at my brother's house and lived in the attic despite the 110-degree temperature in the torrid heat of a typical Midwestern summer. I survived a couple of months there before settling in Topeka with the band's sound man as a roommate.

We found ourselves joining the band at the peak of the their success, an established dance band with three successful floor shows. You would think that people who knew us thought we were crazy to leave the NYC music scene for Kansas, but in that time period eastern Kansas, including Kansas City, Lawrence, Topeka, and Wichita, was a hotbed of music, with notable horn groups and local legends Dan Crary, Mike Finnigan, Pat Metheny, Jerry Hahn, Brewer & Shipley, Les McCann, and Kansas all honing their craft.

The Heartland Band's R-rated version of *The Wizard of Oz* was a show stopper, complete with full costumes, strobe lights, smoke machines, and props. Clubs were packed and there were lines out the door to witness the madness. The Cavalcade of Music show was equally as entertaining, an hour-long nonstop musical and nostalgic journey back through the pop culture of the 1950s and '60s. Finally, a country music show, complete with western garb, which chronicled the history and music through the decades, became a third show option, depending on the type of room we got booked into. Sometimes we'd perform two of the shows on a given night or just play the obligatory five sets of Top 40 dance material.

The Southwest Pub in Topeka became our home base, where we played on a regular basis—six nights a week, five sets a night. Greg, the other guitarist in the band, had taught me some chords back in the late 1960s when he and my brother spent the Christmas holidays with our family in New York City. It was good to reunite with him. After getting a crash course in the Heartland Band material and cutting our teeth at the Southwest Pub we hit the road.

June 1974. The gig at the Red Bull in Johnny Carson's hometown of Norfolk, Nebraska, validated our successes as both a dance band and show band, as both shows were met with warm receptions. One of the regulars at the Red Bull lived a mere football field away from the club and he kindly let us crash at his house, whereby saving us a week of motel bills.

The club owner loved us, and we wound up returning there a few times. On one occasion we drove in two separate vehicles from Topeka to Norfolk, about an eight-hour haul. The lead vehicle broke down on a desolate two-lane highway in Nebraska at around 3 a.m. in the dead of winter. No other car or truck passed by them for nearly two hours, this being the days long before cell phones. They were stranded there with no heat in their broken-down vehicle, huddled together to keep warm. Finally a trucker passed by at around 5 a.m. and called for help on his CB radio. Unfortunately, the second vehicle that I was in, had taken a different route there, so we didn't hear about their near hypothermia fate until we met up in Norfolk.

The Red Bull, Norfolk, Nebraska, 1974

July 1, 1974. After one night at the Moody Blue Club in Iowa City we were promptly fired because we weren't loud enough, even after turning our volume knobs on our amps up to "11," an aberration I would surely never encounter again in my gig history. Our quintet, which consisted of two guitars, keyboards, bass, and drums, with an omnipresent three-part harmony, would typically get the obligatory "turn it down" memo from either a manager, bartender, or owner. In this case the owner, Harry Ambrose, gave us a hand cue to turn it up during our opening set. Yes, it was a large two-decked beer joint, but to have a club owner tell you to increase the volume is as common as Haley's Comet orbiting the planet. After the adjustment it still wasn't good enough. By the third set he had raced out from his office a few times, urging us to play louder. After the gig he summoned us to his office where he promptly fired us. In stunned disbelief we barked back at him in not-so-polite verbiage, expressing the injustice of his action. After all, we had a one-week contract there. However, he could've cared less and told us to pack up and get out of there.

The next day we called our agent back home, who suggested we show up the following night to play anyway. Upon our arrival we found all our equipment stacked up on the side of the stage and a bunch of young rockers in rag tag attire setting up their Marshall amps, double bass drum kit, and gargantuan speaker columns. On our unexpected early road trip back to Kansas we filed our grievance with the musician's union. Eleven months later we received the news of our fate: Mr. Ambrose had filed for bankruptcy. My spirits were lifted, however, after we got booked to play a club in Pittsburgh, except that it turned out to be Pittsburg, Kansas, pronounced the same way but without the "h."

November 1974. Legalized gambling was in full swing in Iowa with roulette wheels and blackjack tables permeating throughout most of the clubs. The Aventino Hotel in downtown Sioux City was a prime hot spot for movers and shakers, with music serving as a secondary backdrop. Therefore, my brother, Walt, would occasionally use a hi-tech megaphone for our shows when he wanted to get the audience's attention over the usual nightclub din; it was highly effective to say the least.

One evening, in our boredom between gigs, he pulled out his megaphone in the hotel elevator and announced that he was Sergeant Kelly and that there was a man with a hatchet loose in the hotel. He underestimated the ease at which his voice traveled through the old walls of the hotel. Minutes later we realized that most of the guests began a panicked evacuation onto the street. Soon the hotel security tracked us down and we admitted our guilt. Fortunately, the unintended prank didn't terminate our gig, Thankfully, they found a bit of humor in the incident once all was said and done.

December 6, 1974. The brutal reality of road gigs in the Midwest set in when we played a one-night frat party at Kansas University in Lawrence. We packed up our equipment and headed out at 2 a.m., faced with a nine-hour haul to Yankton, South Dakota, for a convention gig the next night. On top of long driving distances between towns, there was always the imminent danger of driving in unforgiving climate conditions—from hail storms, blizzards, and devil dusters to scorching heat and torrential downpours.

Upon our arrival, with no sleep to speak of and a quick glimpse of the nearby landmark where Jesse James pulled off one of his infamous train rob-

Heartland Band: (l. to r.) Marc Sussman, Wayne Riker, Joe Meador, Greg Gucker, Walt Riker

beries, we tested our mics with the words "resting 1 2 3" as opposed to the usual "testing 1 2 3." While setting up in this cavernous ballroom, a gentleman who looked like Eddie Munster approached the stage while we were testing our strobe light. Astoundingly, he stood directly in front of it, nary a foot away for a good 30 seconds, as his pointed ears created a giant silhouette on the entire back wall of the ballroom.

March 1975. Our new agent sounded like the real deal, but as you learn over time in the music business you should never get your hopes up for everything to go as planned in all aspects of the business. Almost every room we were sent to was a house of horrors beginning with the Club Eldorado in Waterloo, Iowa. A spacious club with low attendance each night, it was a relatively innocuous gig until we decided to do our *Wizard of Oz* show. Usually accustomed to some form of a somewhat comfortable back room to change into our elaborate costumes, we discovered that the only space available was a four by six-foot utility closet filled with mops, brooms, and disinfectants. The few there didn't seem enthralled by the show anyway, so it was back to Doobie Brothers tunes and "Play That Funky Music" the rest of the night.

Next stop was the Rescue Point in West Des Moines, Iowa, a two-week gig in a hardcore neighborhood bar, complete with a half-dozen pool tables and dartboards, another wrong room for a show band. To make matters worse, nightly fights broke out during our dance sets. In one ugly incident, two patrons engaged in fisticuffs. While they were brawling, we turned on our 1,000 watt arc light that we used in our shows, illuminating the entire club as if it were the second coming.

Foolishly, we attempted our *Wizard of Oz* show. Quite humiliating with no changing room in sight, I had to change into my good witch Glinda costume next to two dudes playing eight ball. Our country show seemed to have a bit more success until a guy at a front table took offense that we introduced Merle Haggard as "America's favorite convict." Unfortunately, it was I who came out wearing a hard hat to sing "Okie From Muskogee." He started yelling out obscenities at me; it was one of the longest three minutes of my life. It seems we struck a nerve with him and assumed that he, more than likely, could relate first-hand to the convict pronouncement.

April 1975. A one-week engagement awaited us on to the opposite side of Iowa in the northwest corner, the heart of the Bible Belt, at the Gallery in Hull, Iowa, population 1,800, with 23 churches within the town limits. Upon our arrival we got turned away from a nearby motel on account of our motley appearance, even though the place had numerous vacancies. We eventually wound up staying in a converted couple of rooms attached to a couple's apartment they rented out.

While setting up our gear in the daytime, two regulars at the bar were jousting around when suddenly they started chasing each other in circles, dumping beer on each other. I could have sworn they were the same two guys in the backwoods scene in the movie *Deliverance*.

On the first few nights we wound up playing to the backs of patrons engaged in blackjack and shooting pool in an upstairs section of the club. In addition, we were informed that there would be nobody in the club on the Thursday, because that day was designated as "church night," with most of the town's people attending services at one of the 23 churches. At the end of our six nights at the Gallery, the club owner informed us that he had no money to pay us for our week's work. It was *déjà vu* soon afterward, when we found out he claimed bankruptcy. Hence, we were never compensated.

Back on the road and finally in a somewhat familiar civilization, we arrived in Macomb, Illinois, home of Western Illinois University and the Gridiron Lounge, a refreshing change from the endless string of dreary bars and being the wrong band in the wrong place. Although we had some lively audiences and dancers, we were contracted to play seven sets a night with an evening set from 5 to 7 p.m., followed by an 8 p.m. to 1 a.m. block. No rest for the weary.

May 1974. Heading next to Woody's Lounge in Gulfport, Illinois, we discovered that the town wasn't on any of our road maps, so we called our agent from a phone booth. He told us that the town exists and to just ask around. At a gas station an attendant said that we were close by and that it was a few miles down the road. He also confirmed that the town wasn't big enough to be on a map. Sure enough, we came upon the welcome to Gulfport sign, population 220, all of whom were living in a montage of trailer parks surrounded by strip clubs along the Mississippi River.

When we arrived at Woody's Lounge we immediately realized that our two dynamic shows wouldn't play well here, especially when we learned that we were competing with Tiny Brooks, a 350-pound stripper who performed in between sets. She lived out of her car as she toured as a stripper around the states; we became fast friends as misery loves company in the harsh reality of the music and entertainment business. Again, here we were, five creative and talented musicians with intelligent shows and snazzy attire, playing at another dive bar to disinterested clientele in the lowest depths of society.

To make matters worse we were put up in a one-room apartment with two beds. Three of us wound up sleeping on the floor. There was an adjoining laundromat with a jukebox, of all things, inside the facility. The school bus stop was directly in front of the apartment as well. Usually crashing after our gig at around 4 a.m., we would be awakened each morning at around 7:30 a.m. by chattering school kids and a repetitive spin on the jukebox of Harry Chapin's "Cats in the Cradle."

On one of our days off we discovered a club on the other side of the river in Burlington, Iowa, called Pzazz, a high-end club in the mold of a swanky Las Vegas hot spot with lavish decor and high rollers pulling up in fancy cars. The irony was obvious: that's the club we should have been playing at. All we could do was shake our heads and soak in the injustice of the music business with the harsh realization that booking agents have no empathy for where they send their bands, as long as they get their commission...

Back home in Kansas we occasionally played at Broadway Ralph's in Topeka. It was an 18-and-up club, where only 3.2 alcohol-content beer was served. These "3.2 clubs" were very popular as 18 to 20-year-olds could drink legally and hear their favorite bands. Most of these poorly constructed plywood establishments had crappy wiring, so it was not uncommon to overload circuits with high-powered amps and P.A. systems. One particular night we wound up blowing fuses seven times during our shows. In the middle of each outage our bass player, Joe, ran to a back boiler room to flip the circuit switch back on.

By the summer of 1975, Marc had moved back to the Big Apple and Greg left the group, so the once highly popular and iconic Heartland Band reformed as a quartet, adding a female singer named Lori. Once you've reached high visibility and star status in your local locale, most of your fans never adjust well to personnel changes, so the band slowly faded into the sunset, playing a few high school dances, a gig in Columbus, but oh no, not Ohio, but rather Columbus, Nebraska, with our final gig at a Kansas State University sorority bash at an Elks Club in Manhattan. No, not New York City, but Manhattan, Kansas.

Wayne Riker

Band #8: American Dream

At the time that the Heartland Band was morphing into its new lineup, I got the opportunity to play for a week with the band American Dream during the first week of August 1975. They were a popular Topeka horn-based band that was on top of the current Stevie Wonder songbook, Average White Band, and Tower of Power, with a mix of some of the emerging jazz fusion tunes, from Chameleon to Little Sunflower. Gary, who fronted the band, provided the soulful lead vocals and electric piano chops and was more than generous in having all the horns and myself take lengthy solos.

Wayne Riker, Topeka, Kansas, 1975

On our break one night we noticed that Susan Ford was in attendance, the daughter of then-President Gerald Ford. She was an intern at the Capitol building that summer. The only problem was that she was 18 years old, and the Southwest Pub was a 21-and-up club; obviously, the bouncers looked the other way, knowing her status.

During the first set on the last night of the gig, I was pleasantly surprised to see two women at a table in front of me, staring intently at every move I made on the fretboard. I immediately assumed they had to be musicians. When

House on 17th St. and Washburn in Topeka, Kansas—$95 monthly rent—where I would practice 12 hours daily as well as giving guitar lessons.

I approached them at the end of the set, thinking they would comment on all my hip chord extensions and use of the Mixolydian mode, they asked me, "We were wondering, is that a bass guitar you're playing?" Lesson learned, never assume anything the audience is thinking when they are watching you play; it's usually the cool shirt you're wearing that garners their attention, not the musical intricacies on your instrument.

Wayne Riker

Band #9: The Carl Johnson Orchestra

In December 1976, an opportunity arose to play in Carl Johnson's Big Band, which proved to be my first chance to wear a very different hat in the commercial gig world. My obsessive practicing was starting to pay off; I was learning from dozens of instructional books, including ones by Mickey Baker, Joe Pass, Ted Greene, and Johnny Smith, and becoming skilled at all my chord usages inside and out, while teaching students out of my house during the day and jamming with anyone who was game at night, in between a steady flow of gigs.

Bob Hope

Bob Hope was coming to town and we were hired to be his band for a couple of shows in Topeka. Legendary fashion designer Edith Head was his "opening act," displaying many of the famous outfits she designed for many a Hollywood star. At rehearsal Hope's musical director called me out for rhythmically overplaying one of the charts, my first indoctrination of staying steady on beats two and four on the swing charts.

At show time his director guided us through Hope's routine, interspersing his classic one liners with his musical numbers. Suddenly, around the midway point of the show, the piano dropped out and it was just guitar and voice. I looked up and saw Hope smiling down at me as he was singing the bridge section of "Tie a Yellow Ribbon 'Round the Old Oak Tree." Never did changing from a C to an Em chord feel so heavy in my hand as ten thousand-plus in attendance looked on in the Topeka Civic Auditorium.

Edith Head

Band #10: The English Version

The English Version: Forrest Bethel, Wayne Riker, Walt Riker, Dave English

Dave English was a dynamic singer; he could sound like David Gates one minute and David Clayton-Thomas the next. People were always blown away that an angelic voice could be produced from a fellow whose weight at times reached nearly a quarter of a ton. At the dawn of 1976, my drummer brother, Walt, and I were recruited by Dave to join his group after the demise of the Heartland Band.

We had a great house gig at Kennedy's Claim in Manhattan, Kansas, our main steady house gig where we played many of the funk and disco classics two or three times a night as "the bump" was quickly replacing all the other dance crazes. When Dave started going to Weight Watchers, he dropped quite a bit of weight. Each weekend there would be a drum roll and he would announce his new weight, eventually paring down to a slender 250 pounds.

Wayne Riker, Topeka, Kansas, 1976

Many of our other gigs were at the Officer's Club at Fort Riley in Junction City, Kansas, another "short drive" from our home base in Topeka. It was a refreshing change of pace—not to be constantly on the road—and we enjoyed a steady diet of gigs within the state. Dave's mesmerizing voice and entertaining skills always guaranteed us callbacks from any club we played.

In Topeka a new club called Mr. Magoo's opened that year, quickly becoming a hot spot for the singles scene and other local musicians to hang. Rich Williams, guitarist for Kansas, frequented Mr. Magoo's when home in Topeka. He swore he'd take some jazz guitar lessons from me, but I'm still waiting to hear from him although we had some great after-hours ramblings about the music scene at Poor Richard's Restaurant in downtown Topeka, the after-hours grub place for area musicians.

Our New Year's Eve gig at Fort Riley on December 31, 1976 was our final gig and would be the final gig I would play with my brother, Walt, until we would reunite 36 years later in San Diego, playing together on my CD, *Guitar Decathlon*, in 2012.

Band #11: The Joni Lee Group

Joni Lee with her dad, Conway Twitty. Photo by Ron Newcomer.

I had never heard country music until I moved to the Midwest back in 1974 other than when I was a kid with my transistor radio, trying to pick up baseball games from other cities while I was standing on the rooftop of my Bronx apartment. In and out of chaotic static I would hear glimpses of "hillbilly" music from radio station WWVA out of Wheeling, West Virginia.

Luckily, when I had joined the Heartland Band in 1974, the other guitarist Greg, while in the process of working up our country music show, suggested I buy two albums: *Greatest Hits of Hank Williams* and *Bob Wills*. It paid big dividends as I locked myself in my room and learned as many classic country licks and tunes as I could, with both of those iconic country artists having a wealth of great players in their bands to steal musical phrases from.

So when Conway Twitty's daughter, Joni Lee, came through Topeka to promote her new album and hit song in 1977, I confidently agreed to step into her band when her

Second Base Club, Topeka, Kansas

Wayne Riker

guitarist couldn't go on tour with her. I only had a day to prepare, but luckily her set included some of the Linda Ronstadt songbook and some standards that I knew. It was the first of many gigs to come down the pike where the bass player was in your ear calling out each approaching chord if you didn't know the tune. The gigs went well but unfortunately her career as a country singer was somewhat short lived, but my brief stay in her band was another confidence builder in achieving my goal of wearing as many different hats as I could on my unlikely musical journey.

Band #12: Twin Guitar Special

Wayne Riker and Dave English, 1977

At the dawn of 1977, with both of us single and no family commitments, Dave English and I decided to take off on our own as a duo and travel the continent for two years with no home base or bills to pay, just an endless six-night, five-set grind nonstop. It was the age of the dreaded drum machine coming into vogue, and we took full advantage of it. We compiled a list of around 200 songs, everything from bluegrass to disco, honing our act by playing a number of local gigs in Topeka before hitting the road.

During that time a luncheon gig at the American Legion proved to be the ultimate "turn-it-down" gig of all time. We wound up playing our electric guitars without amps, and we were still too loud, granted the youngest person in the room was no less than 80 years old. To make matters worse the manager wrote us a check for $150, even though the contract read $250. He claimed the number two on the contract was actually a one in his bastardized cursive writing style. After a six-month dispute through the musician's union, we won the case. So much for the local scene; we found an agent and set sail on the road.

May 1977. In Brush, Colorado, population 3,000, we got a gig at the

Scotch & Steer Bar. They hated us and heckled constantly; there were few dancers and the drunker they got, the more tortuous each minute was. It was back on the carousel paying dues in small town bars, with another agent sending a band randomly to wherever a commission could be secured.

June 1977. Junction City, Kansas, the Fantasia Club in this military town was one of the many strip clubs, which meant more long nights in a rowdy and chaotic setting. At week's end it was break down and load, followed by a sweltering 22-hour drive through the oppressive Midwest heat—100-plus degrees accompanied by our two cats that we traveled with, throwing up most of the way to our next gig in Williston, North Dakota, arriving just in time to set up and play five sets with no sleep. The nearest motel with a vacancy was ten miles out of town and the nearest late-night eatery was 20 miles west at the Montana border at a diner next to the State Line Bar where fights were breaking out in a mini Civil War between folks from North Dakota and Montana

September 1977. Big John's in Salina, Kansas, was an oasis on the plains of central Kansas, a lush and lavish restaurant and bar on a par with a Las Vegas hot spot, a stage over six-feet high that had room for an orchestra. There were free meals and drinks, a rare commodity for any working musician. It was a well-deserved gig after weeks of traumatic road horrors. All that being said, it was time for a new agent. Bill Rothe was based out of Milwaukee. When we met with him he drilled us on business savvy on all levels, right down to matching socks. We were now at his mercy for the next year.

November 1977. Burlington, Wisconsin, the Burlingshire Resort was located on tranquil Brown Lake—nice accommodations and a popular spot for Chicagoans to escape city life. With snow everywhere, most of the residents drove to the club in their snowmobiles. We played most every weeknight to the bartender and candles flickering on the empty tables, although the town would pack the place on the weekends. Good people, good times, and great hospitality from the management—one of those rare moments on the road where you felt right at home. Wisconsin was also an 18-and-up drinking state, meaning that a more youthful crowd would pack the local watering holes. We would return there on two more occasions.

Next up was a grueling 16-hour drive to Thunder Bay, Ontario, where we experienced icy roads, swirling snow, and two-lane roads so narrow you'd swipe side mirrors with passing semis. Upon our arrival at the Canadian border we were detained while inspectors took inventory of our equipment. In the meantime, we had to fill out the proper paperwork to work in Canada, an unwelcome nuisance, although I still have a Canadian social security card they issued to me a few months later in the mail. The final three-hour drive along Lake Superior was harrowing, avoiding herds of deer coming out of nowhere across the barren highway.

Upon our arrival at the antiquated Shoreline Hotel, the temperature was 60 below zero with a wind chill of 110 below zero. It was a dismal looking bar, and we played to disinterested fisherman and locals. We spent both of our birthdays over the two-week hiatus there and had to settle for a funky downtown Chinese Restaurant on Thanksgiving Day, which we later discovered is celebrated in October, in Canada, not November.

We risked our lives on our one day off, driving 20 miles out of town to see historic Kakabeka Falls, where we slid on ice patches and braved brutal gusting winds on foot, just to get up close and snap a couple of photos on my Kodak 110 pocket camera. We were never so glad to get back to the U.S. once the gig ended.

December 1977. Yes, the "Welcome to Minnesota" sign never looked so good, but a 14-hour drive to Marinette, Wisconsin, situated in the northernmost part of the state, was looming ahead. The Dome Cabaret, another resort, was waiting for us, with more snow falling, frozen fingers, and treacherous driving. The bar was lovely, although we were nestled in a corner space inside the circular bar, competing with the roar of blenders that drowned out our vocals every time a blended drink was ordered. Lucky for me, our one day off each week was a Sunday, so hello Lambeau Field for a Packers game two hours south in Green Bay. We bought $5 tickets from a scalper and sat on the frozen ice caked on top of the bare bleacher seats in ten-degree weather, witnessing a season-ending meaningless game against the Lions.

Shoreline Hotel, Thunder Bay, Ontario, 1977.

My sports-related luck continued when we arrived for a one-week gig at the Left Bank Club in South Bend, Indiana, just footsteps away from the Notre Dame University campus. Although there was no football game that week, I got to take lots of photos around the campus. The club was more like a student lounge, with comfy chairs and couches surrounding the bar. A pleasant week of playing background music where few were listening was perfect.

January 1978. In Michigan City, Indiana, the great blizzard of 1978 had struck during our six-week engagement at the local Holiday Inn. Forty-one inches of snow fell over a two-day period, which trapped us in our hotel room for two days with snowdrifts blocking our outside motel door. Semi trucks were buried under snowdrifts and stranded motorists were all crashed in the motel lobby; it was another of many atmospheric episodes amid the worst winter the Midwest has ever seen.

Junction City, Kansas, 1977

April 1978. At the Waterfront Inn in Dixon, Illinois, aka "mafia Tony's club," we had a seven-set gig from 7 p.m. to 2 a.m. with a two-hour dinner set, followed by a five-hour dance set when the "younger crowd" came in. Illinois had a 19-and-up legal drinking age for beer and wine consumption only. We had heard stories about Tony, few that were good, but it turned out to be a great situation. He liked us and appreciated our ability to keep his clientele dancing and drinking.

At the first night's end, Dave, myself, and two women we met were the only ones left before closing. Tony threw us the keys and said lock it up, leaving us there with our living quarters conveniently adjacent to the lounge and connected to the restaurant's kitchen, with a back entrance to a liquor store, all at our disposal 24/7. It turned out to be one the few highlights of our road excursions.

Later in the month, while playing a two-week gig at a Holiday Inn in Freeport, Illinois, one of the customers talked us in to playing a gig at a tractor sale in Pecatonica, Illinois, population 1,200, on our day off no less. Not sure anyone listened to us, as we were window dressing for perspective tractor buyers, but we assumed the tractors enjoyed the music.

May 1978. Pine River, Minnesota, population 860, way up in northern Minnesota was our next gig, a bar/restaurant that really didn't care or need to have a band; it seemed they would be better served with a jukebox. Behind the stage was a big banner stating that the band would be charged a fee if ASCAP or BMI published music was played, which encompasses all music that isn't your own, a fee that the club owner usually pays. In this case it was a memo to the band to have our booking agent cover the fee. At least he was courteous enough to warn us about two women that appear regularly on the first night of each new band's gig, giving us a head's up about not getting involved with them or we'd be headed for penicillin shots down the road. We survived the primitive sleeping quarters in what was a dilapidated cabin, half sinking in a swamp. We made the best of everything and headed back south to our next place of employment.

July 1978. At the downtown Sheraton Inn in Joliet, Illinois, we had a long one-week gig playing to the backs of a dozen drunks at the bar. The club was a tomb. One couple actually showed up on a weekend night and danced; we couldn't thank them enough. A few times each night some of the locals at the bar would play the jukebox while we were on stage playing. No big deal. Play on, ignore, and make sure you got paid at week's end. We never left our hotel rooms during the week, judging by the neighborhood activity down below our seventh story window. It was a wise decision..

Next up was Jumer's Castle in Bettendorf, Iowa, a very cool hotel, restaurant, and bar, complete with banquet rooms and, yes, shaped like a castle. It was definitely a step up from our usual run-of-the mill rooms although we were situated in a piano bar round, a perfect vehicle to be pestered by patrons sitting a foot or two in front of you, yet again having to survive the sound of blenders and loud conversations all around you. President Jimmy Carter's brother, Billy, was one of the regulars. Besides being three sheets to the wind, he was fairly civil to us, mainly requesting a number of obscure cry-in-your-beer country tunes that we didn't know.

August 1978. At the Holiday Inn in Fairmont, Minnesota, every Monday was ladies night. Little did I know I'd meet my future wife there on the second Monday of our two-week gig. She said she was from a place called Chula Vista, California.

October 1978. When we arrived at our next gig at the Kahler Motel in Hibbing, Minnesota, before even unloading our equipment, we made a beeline to the childhood home and high school of Robert Zimmerman, who one may know by his more recognizable moniker, Bob Dylan. Other than the Iron Interpretive Center, a side trip to Fort Frances, Ontario, and watching an ex-

Lambeau Field, Green Bay, Wisconsin

citing World Series that year on the bar's television, it was a routine gig without any particular horror stories.

We finished up our two-year run back at a few clubs in Kansas and parted ways. Over the years Dave and I spoke by phone, reminiscing about all the ups and downs we had experienced and lived to tell about. Our last conversation was in 1997 shortly before Dave's death at 45 years of age.

Band #13: Branded

Wayne Riker

I took a year off from gigging, in 1979, to attend the Guitar Institute of Technology in L.A., feeling like I needed to strengthen some areas of my playing; it was an invaluable year of filling in the necessary blanks as a player and teacher. The staff was a who's who in the music scene, including founder Howard Roberts, Tommy Tedesco, Pat Martino, Joe Diorio, Don Mock, Howard Alden, Les Wise, Al Bruno, Kimbo Smith, and Ron Eschete, to name a few.

Upon arriving in San Diego in 1980, now married and ready to resume my band follies, I didn't know a soul. I grabbed the *Reader*, a local rag that was the main resource at the time for "guitarist wanted" ads in the classifieds. I stumbled upon a country band looking for a lead guitarist. The two women singers fronting the band auditioned me in their modest house in the Mira Mesa neighborhood of the city. Once hired, I realized that both women were "part timers" with less-than-desirable voices. The other band members were decent—a veteran pedal steel guy along with an adequate drummer and bassist.

The two women didn't do much vocal justice to most of the country music standards, but we survived our first gig at the Su Casa Restaurant in Seaport

Guitar Institute of Technology graduation, Los Angeles, September 1980

Village without a hitch, although a short-lived fuzzy feeling when, after two sets at our next gig at Le Chalet in Ocean Beach (currently called Gallagher's), we were asked to pack it up, politely fired midway through the scheduled gig.

Anticipating our next gig at the Catamaran Hotel in Mission Beach, a well-respected high-end musical venue, I held my breath as we meandered through three sets. Lo and behold, we didn't get fired; perhaps their singing wasn't so bad after all. The following gig at the Lakeside Hotel in Lakeside, east of San Diego, came with warning from a few acquaintances, who said to be prepared for nightly fights, with some patrons brandishing weapons. It was definitely an accurate portrayal, but we weren't there long enough to find out, as we were fired again, this time after one set.

That was the last straw as I put in my immediate notice that I was moving on, although they talked me into one last gig, a Christmas party at the Kona Kai Hotel on Shelter Island. Unbelievably, on that night, the phone rings at the hotel's main desk with the news that the two woman singers, the bass player, and pedal steel guy, were all detained in a holding cell at the police station for driving a car that had a past warrant for inadequate equipment operation and that they wouldn't be able to make the gig. The next thing I knew, I was looking out at 200 guests all dressed in formal attire, expecting a six-piece band to provide entertainment at their much-anticipated Christmas gala.

The drummer, Jesse, and I sprung into action, Having no P.A. system, I rushed to the front desk and summoned a microphone and had them run it through the house system of the ballroom. I told Jesse to hang on and follow me—I'm going to pull every dance-able song I can think of out of the woodwork, vocally and instrumentally. I entertained the crowd as if nothing was

The Lakeside Hotel

out of the ordinary, even though by now everyone knew of the existing calamity. As a duo reduced to just guitar and drums we pounded the crap out of our instruments through three sets in the cavernous ballroom before the gentleman that hired us mercifully said we could forego the last set. He paid us in full and thanked us for our effort and for saving the night. So much for my first band adventure in San Diego.

Band #14: Fancy Pants

Fancy Pants: Wayne Riker (far right)

After a few months in San Diego and one failed band, the networking process began. Jesse, the drummer in Branded, knew of a husband-and-wife duo—Fred and Sally—who were starting up a Top 40 band. It was nice to be back in a veteran band with Fred's strong keyboard playing and Sally's powerful lead vocals. It didn't hurt that they had savvy booking skills as well.

Our first gig was in Encinitas on New Year's Eve, 1980 at a haunt called La Costa Cantina. It was my first time exploring San Diego's North County, as we also rehearsed in a house on Encinitas Blvd. Fred introduced me to Fidel's in Solana Beach, a top-notch Mexican Restaurant I'd be visiting for decades to come. It would also be my initial introduction to the fluctuating dynamics of working with a husband-and-wife team, realizing quickly that it was them against us, so to speak, as far as musical and business decisions. Often in these scenarios the pair becomes one all-controlling force.

We landed a house gig at the Jolly Roger in Seaport Village, a corporate chain restaurant. It was a very pleasant ambiance with a great ocean view, complimentary dinners, and pleasant crowds, comprised of locals and tourists alike. It was one of the few times you got a paycheck in the mail with taxes and such taken out. My goodness! It almost felt like a "real" job—I was actually on a payroll. A good thing didn't last long because Fred and Sally decided to hit the road as a duo again, and so it was on to taking that next right or left turn to whatever band would be next.

Wayne Riker

Band #15: The Sally Dunn Orchestra

Wayne Riker

As I was teaching guitar and networking for my next band concurrently, an unassuming woman entered an adult extension guitar class that I was teaching in East San Diego during the spring of 1981. She pulled me out of the classroom for a couple of minutes and asked whether I was available to play guitar in her group. I thought oh, no, what am I getting myself involved in? She was definitely in her 50s or 60s and looked like your typical school librarian. She handed me her business card, which read: Sally Dunn Orchestra... music from Miami. Little did I know that this connection would take me on a musical journey into the world of "casuals" or club dates as they were called back on the East Coast, one-time events from weddings to bar mitzvahs to corporate parties. It turned out that her husband, Herbie, was the sax player in her group and had played with all the high-profile big bands in the Miami area. Sally, an accomplished pianist, had already done her homework around town and hired many of the local San Diego heavyweight horn players.

I quickly realized that I was the "young kid" hired to cover the obligatory rock tunes for the private functions she booked. Almost everyone in her orchestra were twice my age and top-shelf veteran players; they became my role models musically and inspired me to be like them when I reached their age, bouncing around the stage with exuberant energy and enjoying whatever style of music they were asked to play.

Milt Raynor on trumpet and Bob McKewen on clarinet were San Diego legends; they could play most any tune on the spot. The sets would meander at lightning speed with one tune segueing into another, never knowing what the next tune would be; it was simply a hand signal from Herbie for the new key, a solid fist in the air was the key of C, fingers pointing down for flat keys, pointing up for sharp keys. If you knew a tune, great, if you didn't, you did your best to hear the chord changes on the spot. It was the ultimate ear training experience, a gig scenario that challenged you at every turn.

In addition to playing most every temple in San Diego County, some of the gigs took place in plush five-star hotel settings, from the Hotel Del Coronado to the Sheraton Harbor Island, a nice relief from the multitude of previous dive bar circuit gigs. Ms. Dunn and her "Miami Sound Machine" suddenly bolted the San Diego music scene after only a couple of years here, moving back to Miami, but the musical connections established in her band set the table for me as a first-call guitarist in a future string of similar band settings.

Band #16: The Wayne Foster Group

Now entrenched in the casual gig scene in early 1981, I was recruited to be the guitarist for Wayne Foster, a quite remarkable man. Blind since birth he had built a musical empire that cornered the market throughout Southern California, playing any and all special occasions. He incorporated his whole family into his musical shows, including his wife and daughters out front in dancing, singing, and percussion roles while he led the band from behind his piano. We played many exquisite settings, from the Hotel Del Coronado to Palm Desert country clubs to the Beverly Hilton. You had to play exactly what he wanted to hear or it would be next guitarist up. I never got to play a guitar solo in the four months I was on board, as the nonstop shows would focus on vocal and instrumental melodies, ensemble parts, and horn section riffs.

It was a textbook lesson in how to be successful in the commercial music industry—by playing the appropriate music for the client's occasion, lots of medleys, upbeat stage presence, flashing lights, and keeping the music continuous throughout the night. Foster would play solo piano during all the band's breaks. As boring and rote as these gigs could be from a creative standpoint, you smiled, didn't complain, and enjoyed a much higher paycheck for falling in line with these formula-driven gigs even though you knew your pay scale was a pittance compared to what the band leader secured from his opulent clients.

A revolving door of musicians came through the bandstand, as many had short tenures if they didn't play the exact rhythms or notes Foster wanted to

The Beverly Hilton, Los Angeles, California

hear. On one hand you had to swallow your musical pride; on the other hand you got to see what constituted a successful business model. During a rehearsal at the Musician's Union Hall one evening, Wayne's wife asked the drummer for his sticks, then proceeded to demonstrate the correct rhythm pattern she wanted him to play. You have to be thick skinned in these types of musical outfits, but their formula for success works in that market. Yes, music is a business and you can make a good living from it if you have a full-proof production that gets rave reviews from your clients every time out. For the restless sideman, like myself, there's a time when you move on and extricate yourself from the strict show production rigors, although what a valuable experience playing gigs in the most narrow of musical boundaries.

Band #17: Milt Raynor Big Band

I was still "a new kid in town" and it took awhile before some of the casual band leaders realized that the young kid rock guitarist could also read charts and play some jazz as well, hence my entry into trumpeter Milt Raynor's big band in the latter part of 1981. Milt was quite a character, another East Coast guy who migrated west, so we spoke the same language. He could be a tough bandleader and brutally honest at times but also very encouraging, too. He hired many top-shelf local veteran musicians, including Shep Meyers on piano, trumpet player Jerry Fenwick, Frank La Marca on sax, and Dwight Stone on bass as well as a young drummer named Duncan Moore. Milt's charts were hip, everything from jazz standards to the Crusaders.

Lemon Grove, California

We played a few outside park concerts, which were always fun, in addition to a few high schools, one being Kearny High in San Diego. As we entered to set up the band teacher was in the middle of teaching "Dust in the Wind" to a group of guitar students. Soon afterward, our ten-piece band blew the walls down inside the compact band room, although school gigs are almost always the best of audiences. School-age kids are always hungry to hear any type of pro band perform, especially with the drinking age at 21 in California, there aren't many outlets for teenagers to hear bands. Raynor was generous in giving me guitar solos on almost all the charts, a somewhat rarity for a guitarist in a big band setting. Our final gig was at Serra High School on the east side of San Diego. Although short lived, I knew I'd play with Milt again as sideman in someone else's band.

Band #18: The Continental Orchestra

Temple Adat, Poway, California

I was becoming cemented in the pickup band circuit as a first call guitarist but also being recognized for sounding intelligent in most all styles other than rock. Eugene, the drummer, was the leader of the Continental Orchestra and he hustled gigs like crazy. Aside from playing high roller wedding and party gigs at many of the top hotels in San Diego, he also had the inside track for an abundance of "D minor gigs," a common catch phrase for Bar Mitzvahs and Jewish wedding gigs, as most of the hora dance tunes are in the key of D minor.

I knew my time to shine would come when Eugene would bellow out over the microphone, "Okay, all you people that feel young at heart, we're gonna play some rock 'n' roll." Yet again, another great series of gigs that networked me with many of the best veteran players in town. I wound up playing at virtually every temple in San Diego County, as the yarmulke became yet another hat for me to wear in my ongoing musical sojourn.

Wayne Riker

Band #19: Hey Fever

Hey Fever: Wayne Riker (far left)

It was the tail end of 1981 and the dawn of 1982 as the "urban cowboy" craze was in full swing with yuppies adorning cowboy hats and line dancing at the burgeoning country bars across the county. A few of us on the teaching staff at New Expression Music Shop decided to cash in on the fad before it simmered down. Farley the fiddler was already a fiddling legend with the iconic local group Montezuma's Revenge, and Mike Craig's slapping double and triple-time acoustic bass phrases were second to none.

Calling ourselves Hey Fever, joined by Farley's wife, Laurie, on vocals and a singing drummer, Dave, we hit the top clubs right away. Dennis Caplinger, a dynamic electric guitarist and fellow teacher at our shop, joined forces with the group Country Casanova. Between our two groups we dominated many of the house gigs across the county. With Farley's clogging on tables while tearing it up on fiddle and Mike's ostentatious slapping bass riffs, we packed the clubs. With country music at a crossroads among fans of both contemporary and old school barroom styles, you couldn't miss being warmly received at any honky tonk if you played a mixture of both.

The Mustang Club, across the street from the San Diego Sports Arena, was the popular hot spot and place to be, featuring a combination of country headliners and local bands on their monthly calendar. You were royalty if you were asked to play there; we played there on several occasions. In addition to a lengthy house gig at the Circle D Corral in La Mesa, complete with line dancing classes before our nightly start, we had three memorable concert appearances at Knott's Berry Farm, particularly sweet as we got free passes for all the rides, which we took advantage of on our breaks.

The Big Oak Ranch, located in Harbison Canyon, featured an entire frontier town, with a picturesque stage setting for concerts, a mini Red Rocks-type locale. Every top country act from Merle Haggard to Alabama played there, even future pop star Tiffany performed there as a young teen. On a blistering March day in 1982, we survived the 100-degree heat and put on a great show. Sadly, the Big Oak Ranch closed its doors after Rocky, the owner, shot and killed his son-in-law in what became a high-profile trial in San Diego County. Once the urban cowboy rage began to lose its luster, it was time for me to move on.

Wayne Riker

Band #20: The New Expression Band

Ramona Bluegrass Festival, 1982: (l. to r.) Walt Richards, Don Ridgway, Wayne Riker

An ongoing band throughout the 1980s, the New Expression Band was formed by any and all of the teachers at New Expression Music Shop, the roots music store on Ray Street. The main cast of characters included Walt Richards, Don Ridgway, Gary Francisco, Mark Rounds, Mike Craig, Chris Vitas, Vickie Cottle, Dennis Caplinger, Ken Dormer, Dan Sankey, and Ian Law to name a few of the myriad teachers that taught there. We played every year at the Julian Festival as well as the Ramona Bluegrass Festival, which were both sponsored by the shop for many years.

I got to wear my bluegrass hat on many of these gigs, not my strongest suit but, as always, I prepared myself well in learning the repertoire's idio-

The New Expression Band, Julian, California, 1982

syncrasies. Splinter bands easily formed from the huge pool of teachers that could readily become a backup band or a one-night featured act. The store itself morphed into four different names: The New Expression (1974-1997), The House of Strings (1998-2003), Acoustic Expressions (2003-2006), and Old Time Music (2006-2011).

Wayne Riker

Band #21: Roberta Linn and the Gamblers

The Atlantis Restaurant was just a gondola ride over the San Diego Bay from Sea World back in 1982 when former Lawrence Welk Champagne Lady, Roberta Linn, secured that showroom from Tuesday through Saturday for five years. Surviving as her guitarist for a year was nothing short of a miracle, as musicians in her often eight- to ten-piece band were fired left and right. Everyone exchanged business cards right away, not knowing how long they would be employed. The Musicians Union kept a list of all that had graced the stage at the Atlantis over her lengthy run; the final count was a hundred and six.

The tension on stage was palpable; there would be hand signals behind her back for drum cues, volume control, and reprimanding. One minute you'd be scolded; the next minute you'd be praised. Having worked with many tough love musicians and bullies, I had developed a thick skin for most all stage and band dynamics. Guys would be throwing up outside on breaks, yielding to the pressures on stage. If you were called into her office it was usually the ax falling on your employment. I broke in five bass players and six drummers during my tenure there. One drummer was dismissed after three weeks when one night in the middle of a song he stood up and made a gesture with his middle finger at Roberta. He was unemployed before night's end.

When the band was on it smoked, with a full horn section, violin, and pedal steel guitar covering a full complement of musical styles. There were some great charts and strong fellow musicians. Roberta was gracious in giving us solos and we got to do a half-hour set of anything we wanted before she would make her ballyhooed entrance each night. It was one of the few solvent house gigs around, so a steady weekly paycheck was a welcome ray of sunshine for the surviving members. Every Monday morning at 9 a.m. at a bank in the Bay Park section of San Diego, you'd see most of your fellow band mates lined up to make sure the checks were good from the previous week. If you arrived there at 9:30 a.m., it was likely too late and you were doomed to the bank teller's impending words of "insufficient funds."

She would take a night off occasionally and have a fellow entertainer cover the night. One particular time she had Arthur Duncan fill in, the famed tap dancer from *The Lawrence Welk Show*. At rehearsal he asked if we knew "Back Home in Indiana," a tune he used frequently as his featured tap dance number. Half the band knew it while the other half stumbled through it. He stopped us mid-tune and said, "Play something you know in your sleep." We obliged by tearing into "Sweet Georgia Brown," a tune we played in our pre-show and a classic tap dance favorite. All was good. Lesson learned. Don't fake your way through a tune when a big-time performer is in the spotlight, have your act down airtight.

Eventually, I quit the band, dealing with a mid-life crisis of whether to change careers or not, as I enrolled at San Diego State University and eventually Grossmont College to grab another B.A., this one in journalism. As I've learned in this business, stay strong, never show doubt of your abilities and stay professional on all accounts, avoid whining, complaining, and never burn that proverbial bridge. Hence, when I ran into her a decade later at a fish joint in the Gaslamp District, she called me over to her table. She proudly introduced me to her friends by saying, "This is Wayne Riker, a great guitar player who was with me in my Atlantis night club days." That made that whole experience worth its weight in gold.

Wayne Riker

Band #22: Timepiece

Timepiece: (top row) Ninnie Brown, Jeff Johnson, Bill Wilson. (bottom): Wayne Riker, Brett Houser

From the glowing lights of the Atlantis showroom in a high-visibility band to the low-visibility world of gigs playing all the naval bases in town and the off beaten trail of clubs in Southeast San Diego. Liberated from many a tightly regimented arrangement band, I got to stretch out with lengthy guitar solos at peak volumes, playing through a great funk repertoire from Rick James to the Crusaders and Spyra Gyra to Grover Washington tunes. Even their one country tune, a Merle Haggard number, was one I had played in Hey Fever and knew the lengthy Reggie Young solo note for note.

Bill, our lead singer, was a star in our predictable cycle of club rotations but was daunted by the fact that integrated groups were not quite as well accepted in the mainstream club circuits of San Diego County in the early 1980s, so my two-year stay was relegated to our own little microcosm of clubs, which was fine with us. We were stars from all the rowdy EM clubs to the swankier Officers' Clubs throughout the county. Our bass player, Ninnie Brown, didn't drive, so I became his personal chauffeur. In the process, we became fast and close friends.

At this point I found myself now more of a veteran in band hierarchy and fixed an immediate problem of dead air time in between songs. I whipped them into shape with dance sets that moved through medleys and introduced tunes over musical riffs, turning our dance sets into a 45-minute show format, whereby keeping people active on the dance floor.

Jeff, the drummer, a multi-instrumentalist and music major, wrote all of the charts, which were spot-on accurate with every chord voicing and rhythm. He was an amazingly accurate transcriptionist, particularly having to notate many a complicated funk tune. Timepiece was as good a musical group as I had ever played in at this point, but the phone rang in 1984, and it was from a local group looking for a guitarist. I knew it was an offer I couldn't refuse.

Band #23: Stone's Throw

Stone's Throw: (l. to r.) Wayne Riker, Molly Stone, Will Parsons, Phil Shopoff

Hal Crook was a well-traveled and well-known trombone player who settled briefly in San Diego during the early 1980s. I taught a few students at his jazz school off Mission Gorge Road. The connection paid off when the musical outfit, Stone's Throw, was looking to replace their guitarist and called Crook at his school for a recommendation. After beating out seven others in a series of auditions, I found myself situated in one of the most highly visible and established San Diego groups on the scene.

Wayne Riker and Rosemary Clooney

Their eclectic repertoire, loaded with everything from an 1890's medley to Motown, along with a slew of original tunes was as challenging as I had ever encountered. There was a plethora of jazz and swing tunes, many arrangements garnished in tight three-part vocal harmony. As the only chordal instrument, I had to carry the rhythm section throughout all the eclectic styles, in addition to learning all the written third-part vocal harmonies.

Their mailing list had over seven thousand entries, with computer-generating postcards and fliers for all our gigs, very advanced for the early 1980s. Molly Stone played six instruments and Phil Shopoff played five. With the instrumental versatility and vocal arrangements, I had walked into a ready-made local fan favorite. They were annual award winners at the San Diego Music Awards, then called the Entertainer Awards. The band was in high demand, so a day off was rare and we often played two gigs a day. Every Wednesday and sometimes Friday was our house gig at the Belly Up Tavern, as well as a long-running house gig at Elario's in La Jolla. Lines were out the door for most every gig, from Chuck's Steakhouse in La Jolla to the intimate setting of the Old Time Cafe in Leucadia.

The group's popularity expanded into the Los Angeles area, leading to a concert at the 1984 Olympics in the Olympic Village. A gig in Santa Monica drew the attention of the folks at the Princess Cruise Line. A month later we were playing on the "real" Love Boat, a nine-month gig that took us throughout Mexico, South America, the Caribbean, Canada, and Alaska, where we enjoyed five buffets a day; bathing in the sun; watching glaciers calving;

hobnobbing with sports luminaries Pat Riley, Dick Enberg, Cliff Branch, and Todd Christensen; jogging the decks with Jack LaLanne; having tea with Fred MacMurray; and accompanying Rosemary Clooney in song. Although we played all seven days, the sets were broken up throughout the day. I volunteered to play solo guitar background music for the daily afternoon tea, although we'd always have a few hours to visit all the ports of call when docked.

Stone's Throw at Elario's Niteclub, La Jolla, 1985

One musician on board had a low tolerance for the cramped quarters in the lower decks of the ship's quarters; so, he bailed out in Acapulco after three weeks employment and was flown back to L.A. In addition, a few of the very elderly and passengers in failing health spent their last days on the high seas, figuring it was better to die aboard an elegant cruise ship as opposed to a dismal hospital room stateside. Finally, the nightly midnight buffet was prepared by some of the top European chefs. Being that most passengers were asleep or at the ship's disco, only about ten percent of the feast was consumed. The other 90 percent was dumped overboard, certainly a feast for many unsuspecting sea inhabitants.

A memorable two-year stint drew to a close as my first child was born, so it was back to land and square one as I pulled out the *Reader* to seek yet another gig adventure, soon to realize I was going from the penthouse back down to the basement. As the saying goes, "Always be nice to people on your way up, because you'll see the same people on your way down."

Band #24: Elvis Excitement

Elvis Excitement: Wayne Riker (second from right)

The music business is a survival of the fittest, a psychological roller coaster of ups and downs. If you can hang with the ebb and flow of shifting winds of change, you can survive. Such was the case in 1985. Coming out of one of the most successful bands in San Diego musical lore, Stone's Throw, I found myself back on land a week later, scrolling through *Reader* ads for a new band.

Alas, an Elvis impersonator, whose stage name was Aaron Hart and who was residing in Ocean Beach, was looking for a guitarist. After a brief audition, I got hired, only to find myself going from the opulence of cruise ship life and playing with some of the best musicians worldwide, to the decadence of our first gig behind chicken wire at a biker dive bar in Spring Valley, staring out at 50 dudes in leather barbecuing some crappy looking steaks and heckling us. Not even the dazzling outfits "Elvis" wore could camouflage his marginal vocal ability.

Yes, the music business is a tough business, one never knows who is talking behind your back and plotting your removal from the band!

Gone were the high-profile gigs throughout the jazz clubs in La Jolla and the weekly gigs at the Belly Up Tavern, replaced by infamous hole-in-the-wall clubs named the Outpost, Don's West, Pizza Plus, Happy Days Car Hop, some VFWs, and yes, Little Las Vegas, a converted bowling alley on Palm Avenue in Imperial Beach that was turned into a rental hall for special occasions. Eight months of backing "Elvis," and his less-than-stellar voice, was enough as the band began a mutiny, a common happening in many a band, where four members are huddled in a corner on a break while the fifth member stares over their way, realizing he's not part of the conversation and that a mutiny is imminent.

50 Years • 50 Bands • 50 Bucks

Band #25: Sh-Boom

Sh-Boom: Mike Nelson, Dino Ingram, Wayne Riker, Hoke Simpson

It was 1986 and MADD (Mothers Against Drunk Driving) successfully lobbied Congress to raise the drinking age to 21 for all states and also lower the DUI limit to .08, thus forcing more club owners to scale back bands to weekends as many folks became apprehensive to get into their vehicle on a weeknight to hear live music and face the possibility of a DUI offense. As a result, most all our gigs were on weekends. The mid-1980s saw a huge wave of bands going into the "oldies" market as the 1950s and '60s rock music was

Sh-Boom: Wayne Riker (passenger seat)

becoming vintage, so we built our repertoire strictly around that era and named the band Sh-Boom, after the hit song in the early 1950s.

I put together a slick promo package and hit the streets to book the band, culminating in a three-year run of steady work. After a rehearsal one day, we strolled into Wear It Again Sam, a vintage costume shop on Park Blvd. in San Diego, spotted four leopard-skin jackets and knew we had eye-catching outfits for the stage, even though we knew the ostentatious jackets would be high-brow attire for many of the blue collar neighborhood bars we'd wind up playing at.

We became the main house band at the Horseshoe Lounge in Lemon Grove, a town just east of the city limits of San Diego, claiming to have the

50 Years • 50 Bands • 50 Bucks

The Silver Fox, Pacific Beach, San Diego, 1987

"best climate on earth," indelibly printed on the giant lemon in the center of town. The club had just been bought by a new owner, Dirk, who changed the image from a tough biker bar to a popular dance destination with lively oldies bands.

A month into our steady gig there, a new bartender, who barely spoke English, had been hired. We took wagers on how long he would last. None of us ever would have guessed that Ivo would still be there 30 years later. With business on the rise, Dirk filmed a TV commercial that ran on KUSI, a local television station, between midnight and 5 a.m, which included us playing in our vaunted leopard-skin jackets. The commercial was filmed during the day, but was made to look like a wild weekend night as he recruited many of the club's regulars to fill the rafters mid-day.

In January 1988, legendary southern California deejay, "Shotgun" Tom Kelly, had set up shop for his live weekly oldies show at the Corvette Diner, a 1950s-style diner in downtown San Diego. We were featured guests on one of his spots. Crowded into a tiny makeshift recording booth, we did a short interview with him, followed by the daunting task of singing *a capella* (singing without instrument accompaniment) on three doo wop tunes. Quite a nerve-wracking experience knowing you're on a live broadcast with little room for error on a mainstream AM radio station.

It was steady work with gigs nearly every weekend, churning out classic rock goodies. I had finally made it to leader status, somewhat by default, as I was now the guy with the most experience in the business, knowing all the dos and don'ts in the process. I was strict in running the band, but by doing things the right way, we procured steady employment for three years, however, playing to "Happy Days" crowds that loved to dance to oldies. A bit of musical boredom eventually set in, and so, sadly, the leopard-skin jackets headed toward the mothballs.

Band #26: Tuxedo

Now halfway through my musical odyssey I was thrown back into the casual gig circuit in 1988, when I got a call from legendary San Diego trumpet man Frank Nelson. Even though now approaching the age of 40, I was still the young hire to cover much of the contemporary guitar stuff.

Frank Nelson

His quartet, Tuxedo, had just finished up a 19-year run at the Stardust Hotel in Mission Valley (now the Handlery Hotel), a long-standing house gig record in the San Diego music annals. Although in his seventies at the time, he had more energy and stage presence than most musicians half his age, along with some great stories from the heyday of jazz in the 1930s and '40s. He had played on *Andy Griffith's Variety Show* in the late 1960s; the famous crumpled cornet he used is on display at the Museum of Making Music in Carlsbad.

I played a lot of classy rooms with him throughout San Diego County, from country clubs to resorts, along with some exclusive 1988 Super Bowl parties. He was one of the few gracious leaders to work for. I got to shine on his jazz and big-band repertoire, although one gig was truly humbling when we played a 50-year wedding anniversary in 1988 for a couple that wanted the band to play all the hit pop tunes from 1938. Frank warned me to lay low in that I probably wouldn't know many of the tunes. He was certainly on point, as I knew none of the tunes throughout the three-hour gig. Luckily, the keyboard player had charts, so I survived somewhat. Playing pop tunes of the day is a far cry from knowing the "jazz standards" of the day. A present day analogy would be like sending a young musician to play a 1960s gig, thinking he or she would ace all the standard tunes (Beatles, Doors, Hendrix,

50 Years • 50 Bands • 50 Bucks

Wayne Riker

Zep, Stones, etc.) but instead encounter a set list from groups such as Unit 4 + 2, the Swinging Blue Jeans, the Buckinghams, the Critters, the Vogues, and the Cyrkle.

It was another great gig experience with veteran musicians and a pleasure to work with true pros once again, who do all the right things to maintain success in making a career of music performance. Once again, though, my phone rang and my unlikely journey was about to take a hard left turn.

Band #27: "Are You Lonesome Tonight" Band

Wayne Riker (far right), 1989

Will Parsons, the drummer from Stone's Throw, contacted me in the summer of 1989 and asked me if I had ever played a musical theater gig. He had played a string of shows at the San Diego Repertory Theater since the early 1980s. I told him I hadn't, but I would welcome the opportunity. The Rep was premiering a show called *Are You Lonesome Tonight?*, penned by an English playwright, a mostly dark play on the life and times of Elvis Presley, which covered the whole spectrum of Presley's vices, from his frequent womanizing to his drug abuse, but also traced Presley's entire musical career in the process.

I brought my guitar along with me to audition for Rep founder Sam Woodhouse, who was also cast in the production as the older Elvis character. I played him a variety of rockabilly licks and quoted a few Presley riffs. Ten minutes later he said, "Okay, you got the gig," but warned me that playing a musical theater gig was very different than playing in a band. The other three musicians, including Will, bassist Oliver Shirley, and keyboard and conductor Fred Lanuza, along with the entire cast, had all done musical theater work in the past. Hence, I was affectionately dubbed "theater virgin" right away.

(l. to r.) Will Parsons, Wayne Riker, Oliver Shirley, Fred Lanuza

Bob Jewett, the musical director, was a very cool cat from the Big Apple who had scored the music for a variety of television shows. He was also a guitarist and appointed me to write basic chord charts for all the tunes in the show. He then asked me if I played slide guitar, and I said yes, although I was a bit rusty at the time. Immediately, my instincts kicked in and, like I've always told my guitar students, "Never tell anyone what you can't do; never show fear." People will figure out what you can or can't do. Never plant a seed of doubt in their minds or they will be cognizant of your vulnerabilities. Accordingly, I spent a solid week working on my slide technique, hoping it would be adequate. It turned out he wanted me to play some down-home

Delta blues slide guitar licks as a backdrop to scenes from Presley's early years growing up in Mississippi.

I used an acoustic-electric guitar tuned to a G chord for just the right effect. In addition, I pulled out my semi-hollow Gibson electric guitar for the rockabilly tunes that Presley did during his earlier years. My country class at the Guitar Institute of Technology, taught by Nashville great Al Bruno, paid off as I incorporated the hybrid picking technique he taught us to replicate the style accurately.

For the later Presley period, I used my Fender Strat for the high-energy rockers. Switching among three guitars for the three distinctive styles in the show was a blast, as was playing to a large attentive and appreciative audience six nights a week, eight shows total, with matinees weekly. I immediately took to musical theater, although Sam was right—it's not like playing in a band, because you have to be right on time and right on the money with all your parts or you'll hear it later from the stage manager or the actors. There's little room for error.

At one of our Sunday matinees a former San Diego Repertory actress was in attendance. It was her birthday, so the cast had a birthday cake awaiting her in the Green Room when the show ended. She complimented the cast on their performance and then came over to me and said, "Hey, guitar man, nice job." It isn't every day one gets a compliment from Whoopi Goldberg.

The show ran six weeks and closed without an extension. It got mixed reviews as most expected an Elvis revue-type show. Many couldn't handle viewing the darker moments of his life. On closing night Jewett had taped the show, later commenting to me that he loved the versatility of my guitar playing, especially my slide guitar phrases behind the early scenes. He said, "Man, you sounded like Ry Cooder!" I smiled and said thanks, never letting on that I was locked in my room practicing slide guitar hours on end for a whole week before opening night.

Band #28: True Grit

Wayne Riker

As 1990 approached I had now gained the reputation of what many call in the business a mercenary or freelancer, a player that can go in on the spot and play a gig on short notice, sometimes for one night or longer. These sub gigs arise for a number of reasons—usually a band member goes on vacation, is ill, or has a sub gig themselves. In any event I had been in town long enough and had played with enough musicians in different genres that performing options arose more and more frequently for me.

True Grit, a working rockabilly-based band, needed a guitarist to fill in for their guitarist Jim, who was headed back East to visit family. Ironically, he was the guitarist that usually was in the guitar chair at the San Diego Rep-but was in Europe at the time *Are You Lonesome Tonight?* opened so, for a second time, opportunity knocked.

I was on board for a couple of weeks with no rehearsals, just a song list with the keys they play the songs in, which were sent to me a few days before the first gig. Most of the songs were ones I either had played or taught to students. When there are a few you may not know it's always best to lay low and use your ears, although most of the songs in that style are somewhat simple chord progressions anyway.

The Waterfront bar, San Diego

A few of the gigs were at the Waterfront, San Diego's oldest bar, situated downtown near San Diego Bay. Although a certified dive bar, the layout was surprisingly hip, with an outdoor section adjacent to an L-shaped bar and eating section. There was no stage, so we played on the floor with only a handful of passersby to the restrooms giving us any lip service. It was, overall, a nice cross section of patrons, from blue collar to downtown executives to artists and actors.

My final gig with them was at the Sycuan Casino, in El Cajon, as the burgeoning casinos around the county were becoming new sources of gig possibilities. Mission accomplished, fun band, easy gig, and as you usually hear, "job well done," as the others in the band always appreciate your effort and time put in to help them out in a pinch.

Band #29: Rival

Wayne Riker, NAMM Show, Anaheim, California, 1995

Tom, the drummer from Sh-Boom, tracked me down in the fall of 1990. Their guitarist was dealing with home and work issues and needed to sub out periodically. It was my next challenge to fit in with another quartet cranking out classic rock and Top 40 material with a week's window to prepare. Bernie, the keyboardist and leader, worked from a precise set list, and I'd have to chase him down at his day job to obtain the current lineup of tunes. Story has it that he got the band name Rival when a client asked him what his new band's name was. Having no definite name yet, he looked around the room and spotted a crock pot with the company name Rival on it, and so it goes.

They had a steady gig at a small restaurant bar called Maxwell's, adjacent to a Days Inn on Miramar Road in San Diego. It was steady weekends for a few months, playing to a friendly crowd of travelers and home town friends. No stage but another designated floor space to squeeze into, facing a makeshift dance floor that was not much bigger than a walk-in closet. Any gig is worth its price in gold when musicians get fed on the house, a luxury that seldom occurs, as many who play in bands find themselves sneaking into a back kitchen to scrounge some leftover rolls.

Campland on the Bay

Bernie would call on me periodically throughout the decade as a fill in. The group name changed to the Ultratones, with some new faces and new tunes. There was a great gig at Campland by the Bay, an outdoor concert stage at Mission Bay, attended enthusiastically by many locals and tourists visiting the San Diego area. There was a second great gig there a few months later, at least I heard it was great, as I wasn't sure I was on the gig because I hadn't received a song list from Bernie. It was a rare moment of miscommunication on my part, and before the days of cell phones and texting, nobody's fault, but I heard Bernie pulled out all the stops, doubling on piano and guitar.

Band #30: Then and Now

You never know what gig may fall into your lap at any time; it's what makes the whole adventure exciting—the exhilarating rush of unknown challenges lurking around the bend. You have to have a certain personality for it and be willing to adapt to a new situation at a moment's notice. My old buddy Will, the drummer, had an inside track on procuring a weekly gig at the world-renowned La Costa Resort in their main ballroom, the Tournament of Champions Lounge.

We recruited our theater cohort Oliver to play bass and hired an up-and-coming piano prodigy, John Nau, along with female vocalist Ria Carey. After two weeks of intense rehearsals Then and Now was born, with an eclectic set list of swing, jazz, Latin, rock, and country standards. Any time you play an upper-echelon lounge gig, it's propitious to have as many styles covered as you can.

The stage was at least eight feet high, a nice bonus because dancers can't fall into your equipment or try to hold conversations with you when you're mid-tune. We pulled the gig off successfully during our month-long run there in the summer of 1990 and waited to see if a future booking would be in the cards for us there.

Band #31: Fahrenheit

Wayne Riker

Shirley was our new female vocalist as we prepped for a return engagement at the La Costa Resort in the fall of 1990, armed with a hip variety of tunes from Aretha Franklin to Bonnie Raitt. It was good news for us when we heard the four-hour night would be only two 45-minute sets, since we alternated with another band, which meant we could hang in a plush downstairs Green Room while the other band was on.

On opening night our lovable pianist, John, forgot to bring his tuxedo and showed up in sneakers and casual dress instead, another classic moment of a musician spacing out on a memo. Luckily, we were able to borrow a white shirt and bow tie from a guy in the other band. John's pants and sneakers were camouflaged by his piano, so we survived what would have been an embarrassing episode.

La Costa Resort and Spa

After a nice run in those cushy surroundings our contract was up and we all moved on. John went forward with eventual gigs with Belinda Carlisle, Hootie & the Blowfish, and Ratt, and I was called back into the world of musical theater.

50 Years • 50 Bands • 50 Bucks

Band #32: The Satanic Mechanics

The Satanic Mechanics, San Diego Repertory Theatre, 1991

The San Diego Repertory Theater came calling again in 1991, this time forming a band for the musical *The Rocky Horror Show*. It was good timing as the popularity of the cult movie was at a feverish pitch at midnight showings across the land. Our five-piece band was given the musical score to take home, followed by a few separate band rehearsals, which led to the impending run through with the actors.

This time around I was ready for the grueling 12-hour tech rehearsals, often refereed to as "tech hell" in theater circles. These rehearsals included a lot of dead time between musical numbers, while lighting, sound, choreography, and stage props were locked in. The cast hailed primarily from New York, Los Angeles, and San Diego, a talented group with impressive acting resumes. Sean Murray, who played Frank N. Furter, coined the band name the Satanic Mechanics, because our outfits somewhat resembled grease monkeys.

Every show was a sellout during the four-month run, eight shows a week, which were sometimes wallpapered with die-hard movie fans whom the theater would let in for free to ensure a sell out. There would be certain obvious moments when the audience would yell back at the actors but nowhere near the

Cast of Rocky Horror Show

chaotic stream of verbal volleys in the movie theaters. Our band was visible on stage, perched high on a platformed tower, stage left, adorned in our silver outer space garb.

Midway through the show our keyboardist and musical conductor, Stu Shames, moved back to Philadelphia and I was anointed bandleader. Here we go again, another challenge. I had to be a quick study in conducting, albeit much simpler setting tempos and giving hand cues for a quintet, opposed to conducting an orchestra. I gleaned through some of my college textbooks

Sean Murray

from some of the elective music courses I took and practiced in the mirror for a couple of days before it was show time again.

In addition to helping out our new piano guy, a new bass player named Kelly Bowen came on board, fresh out of Berklee College of Music, playing one of her first gigs. All pulled through and everything went smoothly. The audiences were great; it was a smash hit and the band was treated like rock stars with people dancing in the aisles and cheering us during the encores.

Band #33: Scary Mary and the Noose

Ed, one of my guitar students, was the lead guitarist for a popular North County group called Scary Mary and the Noose. In 1991, they had a steady weekday gig at the Belly Up Tavern in Solana Beach. He asked me if I could sub for him for one night, a night they were supposed to open for the Desert Rose Band, which featured former Byrds member Chris Hillman and guitar ace John Jorgenson. I accepted and was happy about returning to a familiar stage that I had played on many a night with Stone's Throw.

So there I stood in the green room at the Belly Up, which was once a recording studio seven years earlier, where I recorded *Stone's Throw Live at the Belly Up*. The late, great Malcolm Falk not only ran the studio but he was also responsible for booking many of the eclectic top-shelf acts during the heyday of the club. Now I found myself backstage with Hillman and pedal steel man Jay Dee Maness, swapping stories and trading licks as we were warming up for our respective shows.

After our opening set of country covers and some originals, all memorized via a cassette tape the band had sent me earlier that week, I left the stage with my electric guitar in hand, passing Jorgenson on his way on stage hauling a rack of 12 guitars, quite impressive visually but equally impressive

50 Years • 50 Bands • 50 Bucks

when he played them. At night's end, as all musicians do, you exchange the obligatory compliments to each other, never really knowing how true they may be or not, but that's how it is in the fragility of musical performance and in life itself.

Band #34: Judy Ames and Odyssey

Judy Ames and Odyssey: Wayne Riker (second from right)

Back in 1986, when I was with Sh-Boom, we had auditioned a few tenor sax players to augment our group, a pivotal instrument for playing golden oldies from the 1950s and early '60s. One of them was Judy Ames. She came in with a confident attitude and had prior experience in bands. After a couple of tunes, I suggested we play "Johnny B. Goode." She said, "What key?" I replied, "B flat, although we usually do it in the key of A." I was always aware that sax players preferred flatted keys, particularly in rock-oriented tunes, so I was being courteous. However, she stubbornly insisted that we play it in the key of A and became defensive about it. After some stubborn back and forths, I finally said, "Okay, the key of A, here we go." After the audition, we didn't call her back, as we sensed somewhat of an attitude.

Flash forward to 1992 and recently divorced, I often hit the bar scene, sometimes even singing karaoke. One night the karaoke host looked familiar. It turns out it was Judy Ames. After mutually recounting that awkward audition incident, she told me she was forming a basic variety band, particularly aimed at a connection she had for playing a series of concerts for the impending America's Cup races in San Diego.

She scrambled together the usual quartet configuration of drums, bass, keys, and guitar, positioning herself out front singing and playing sax and flute. A week later we were on stage outside of TGI Friday's on San Diego Bay, playing to the raucous international crowds of sailing fanatics, surrounded by oodles of media coverage. Celebratory crowds are always the easiest to play for, particularly when their team is winning, any music sounds great. The Americans had brought home the Cup, a great moment, but like all moments, the excitement gradually faded away and the adrenalin rush of the next challenge set in.

Band #35: Camille's Commotion

Wayne Riker

October 3, 1992. The setting was the Omni Hotel in San Diego, and a husband and wife duo that I had played with on a few occasions hired me for a prestigious VIP corporate gig. Camille was the lead singer and her husband was the keyboardist, a familiar combination in mine and many others' gig annals. There was a number of political dignitaries present and some well-known names, although I can't recall who they were or what the exact occasion was all about. It matters little as all you're usually told is that there will be "important" people there, so play your best. At this point of my career I was immune to most any stressful scenario; I had been through the ringer and at this point one becomes bulletproof to external stimuli on stage and in the audience.

After an opening set the drummer and I were chatting on our break, comparing notes on working with husband-and-wife duos in our travels, when we were called back for the next set. A few songs into the set and midway through "Freeway of Love" one of Camille's high heels got caught in between two of my effect pedals on my pedal board. Her heel was wedged squarely in between the space and locked in without any wiggle room. There was no way she could extricate her heel, other than removing the shoe, which she couldn't do directly in front of the attentive dignitaries. The show went on and she did her best singing in a stationary position, doing her best Joe Cocker gyrations in order to initiate some semblance of stage presence. The set mercifully ended half an hour later. At the break we had to use a pliers to remove her shoe from the pedal board. The last set proceeded without a hitch, and nobody ever knew the stage predicament we encountered, a lesson you learn in the business: never show your hand in any stage miscues or musical errors, short of an explosion or a drummer playing a shuffle rhythm during a straight eighths tune.

Wayne Riker

Band #36: Tobacco Road

Tobacco Road and Stone's Throw together in concert, Hotel San Diego, 1984

Sue Palmer and I met back in 1984 when I had just started playing with Stone's Throw. Her group Tobacco Road was a sister group, as both groups had a similar horn-oriented sound, while playing a wide variety of jazz tributaries, including swing, boogie woogie, Dixieland, and bop. Both groups had driving rhythm sections, strong lead vocals, and snazzy vocal harmonies. Both our groups were rarely out of work, playing all the hot spots in La Jolla, North County, and Shelter Island. In August 1984, both groups combined forces on stage in tandem for a gala night at the San Diego Hotel downtown, an event we called Hep Cat Holiday, a night of dancing to vintage jazz classics.

Flash forward to November 1993 at the Silver Gate Yacht Club in San Diego, and there I was subbing for Sue in Tobacco Road. The group was still groovin' and swingin' with a couple of new faces in her band. They were certainly bigger shoes to fill when subbing for a pianist as a guitarist, especially having short notice on many of these gigs, but I survived the night, always keeping in mind a valuable tip from a former wise band mate: "when in doubt, lay out!"

Band #37: Ronnie Rebel and the Reunions

Tara and Trent Riker at their dad's theatre gig

In February 1994, another local guitarist recommended me for the vacant guitar chair in a long-running local musical, *Reunion*, a nostalgic but satirical take on the innocence of the 1950s. I had a few days to prepare and one band rehearsal before the curtain went up at the Checker's Theater in the Gaslamp District downtown. The charts were easy and fun to play, standard classic rock ditties. The independent production was a few levels down from the intensity of my previous theater gigs but nonetheless the same high concentration level needed, with no margin for error.

Wolfman Jack

My daughter and son, eight and five respectively at the time, were now old enough to take to work, so to speak, especially because they had no choice in a joint custody arrangement when no babysitters were available. The good news was that they got to hang out in the Green Room, witness rehearsals, and get to see many runs of the same show, a perk for them that would extend into my future musical theater employment as well.

Suddenly, at nearly 44 years of age, it dawned at me that I was now at the crossroads of being a wily veteran and no longer the young kid, validated when I noticed that everyone in the cast, including the band, were all younger than I. During the last two weeks of the five-week run, Wolfman Jack joined the show as the narrator and sang some tunes as well. He had some great stories to tell about his many years in radio and of numerous characters in the entertainment world. He wasn't in the best of health and died the following year. As for me, another musical theater gig was in the books.

Band #38: Dixie Highway Band

Wayne Riker in 1994

After nearly 15 years in the same city, the networking process had grown exponentially, most everyone in the business knew who you are, providing your reputation hadn't been soiled along the way. Bill Doyle, the music director from *The Rocky Horror Show* production I played in, called to hire me for an independent musical theater production called Dixie Highway, with noted director Will Roberson and musical director Steve Gunderson at the helm. The play centered around the everyday life of a family living in the deep South, paralleled with the significant world event of the United States moon landing in the summer of 1969. The range of music was

My cat, Tico (1975-1992), my road companion through 25 states and Canada

loaded with beautifully written ballads and catchy pop-oriented tunes, with a high-level cast of actors and singers that were backed by a quartet of myself, drums, and two keyboard players.

I was back in the trenches of musical theater, six shows a week at the Hahn Theater (now the Horton Grand Theater) in San Diego's Gaslamp District. Again, another intense challenge of utmost concentration in reading the charts and watching for all the cues carefully, there was no margin for errors. The audiences loved the show and respected the high caliber of artistry, but after the seven-week run we were surprised that the show wasn't extended. More often than not, however, shows of high quality with depth and substance tend to go over most people's heads. Akin to music in general, the more watered down and palpable the music is, the more popular it is with the majority of audiences.

Band #39: A Christmas Carol Band

Fred Lanuza, Brenda Spevak, and Wayne Riker in 1996

One proficient job with a musical director often leads to another, so I was reunited with Steve Gunderson during the 1994 holiday season, as he became the musical director for the long-running San Diego Repertory Theater production of Charles Dickens' *A Christmas Carol*. It was to become an annual gig through the holiday seasons of 1995 and 1996 as well, in the same locale at the Lyceum Theater in downtown San Diego.

I was part of a small chamber quartet comprised of violin and two key-

Myche Taylor and Maurice Mendoza

boards, utilizing an acoustic guitar for the lilting Victorian musical score. I was designated to add in percussion parts, incorporating wind chimes, bells, and tambourine accompaniment to embellish the Christmas spirit of the Dickens classic. The pre-show included greeting the audience as they entered the theater and getting them in a festive mood with a selection of holiday classics while we strolled around in our caroling garb.

We played behind a curtain off stage, not visible to the audience, so you had to be alert to the actors' cues audibly. There were often long stretches of time in between guitar or percussion parts, so it was often customary to nap or work on a crossword puzzle before the conductor would get your attention for the next cue. One benefit of a holiday show is that you could always count on the length being one month of steady employment, usually running from post-Thanksgiving to a few days after Christmas. Even though most of the production team would be in good cheer for the holiday season, it didn't negate the fact that we had intense daily rehearsals over a three-week period before previews and opening night.

Wayne Riker

Band #40: The Suds Band

The Suds Band, 1995: (top row) Bill Doyle, Oliver Shirley; (bottom) Tom Versen, Fred Lanuza, Wayne Riker

Shortly after the 1994 *Christmas Carol* production, in mid-1995, a revival of the musical *Suds* was in the works, an original script by Gunderson and actress Melinda Gilb, which started at the San Diego Rep in the mid-1980s and subsequently made it to a run off Broadway in the Big Apple. The brilliantly slapstick follies of the three women, one-man cast, including Gunderson and Gilb, set in a laundromat, took audiences by storm. The musical score included over a hundred songs, all from the 1950s and '60s, some obvious, some more obscure, but all relevant to the ongoing skit-like scenes. We had a full house almost every night of old and new fans of the show

The Suds Cast: Melinda Gilb, Shana Wride, Steve Gunderson, Susan Mosher

throughout the nine-week run, eight shows a week.

After a couple of personnel changes the show got contracted for a two-week stint in January 1996, at the Poway Center for the Performing Arts in Poway, just north of San Diego. I was elevated to musical director and conductor, a fitting end to my theater beginnings as a "theater virgin." In short, whatever you can't do, figure out quickly how to do it without showing any doubt or fear and success will prevail.

Musical theater gigs were a great experience for grace under pressure, playing accurately splices of musical phrases at varying tempos, time signatures, and shifting keys, knowing that any mishaps leave the actors holding the bag out front. The discipline and concentration it takes to play all your parts perfectly at the exact cue times in front of attentive audiences in large auditoriums helped me to fortify a "no fear" attitude for any and all future musical encounters.

Band #41: Bursting at the Seams

Lee, one of my guitar students, persuaded me to join his group in the summer of 1997, needing to fill a vacancy for a lead guitarist. Being a working band with regular gigs most weekends, I accepted. The band's repertoire was a main course of 1970s and '80s Americana rock, including tunes by Springsteen, Mellencamp, the Allman Brothers, and Van Morrison. We played nearly every neighborhood bar in San Diego and, yes, $50 per man at many a classic watering hole, including Rosie O'Grady's, the Office, Tuba Man's, and the Blarney Stone in addition to a few outdoor park concerts.

Bursting at the Seams: Wayne Riker (far right), 1999

John, the bass player, was a strong lead singer, a must for any band playing the cover band circuit; it's the one musical element the audience can discern. It was a refreshing change to get back into a steady band again after a string of musical theater and freelance gigs.

Band #42: The Riker/Heller Duo

Wayne Riker. Photo: Nancy Rank.

In 1998 Rick, a harmonica teacher at the shop where I was teaching guitar, approached me about forming an acoustic blues duo, à la Sonny Terry and Brownie McGhee. It sounded cool, another change of pace. We worked up a solid list of acoustic blues standards, with both of us trading lead vocals, accruing enough tunes to play two sets, the usual quota for most

Twiggs Coffeehouse, San Diego. Photo: Liz Abbott.

coffeehouses.

Our main gig was at an established local San Diego coffeehouse called Twiggs, one of the only coffeehouses at the time that had live music nightly. The performances were held in a separate room from the serving area, a stark concrete space with folding chairs set up in a dozen rows. The majority of attendees were frequent customers there—acoustic music junkies that love their coffee and scones amid the earthy vibe. I was once again fortunate to play to a listening crowd, minus the alcohol consumption, in a compact two-set evening. It wasn't the most lucrative of gigs, but sometimes you can do somewhat well with a small cover charge at the door along with the traditional "passing the hat" for tips.

Band #43: The Shelle Blue Band

The Shelle Blue Band: Wayne Riker (second from right), 2000.

Ninnie Brown was one of the best bass players I worked with when we played together in the early 1980s, but little did I know how good he was on guitar. He invited me to join the Shelle Blue Band as a second guitarist in 1999, in a soulful quartet that backed up R&B vocalist Shelle. Per usual, I was walking into a working band with the daunting assignment of learning a lengthy song list quickly. They had already established gigs in the Gaslamp District at popular haunts that included Croce's Top Hat, the

Adams Avenue Street Fair, San Diego, 1999

Juke Joint Café, and Buffalo Joe's.

It had been a while since I had worked in a double guitar group with another strong lead guitarist, but the advantages are that your solos can be supported better with a rhythm guitar behind you, and when you're both playing rhythm, one guitar can echo bass and horn type riffs. Shelle was generous with giving both of us lengthy solos on most tunes, a luxury in blues bands where longer solos are more accepted with audiences as opposed to shorter formatted solos in cover and show bands.

The regular Monday night gig at Croce's Top Hat, a club opened by Ingrid Croce, wife of the late Jim Croce, drew locals and tourists alike to the centralized hub of live music in the Gaslamp. Adjacent to the club was Patrick's, a long-standing watering hole that hosted blues bands as well. There was an alley that connected the back doors of each club, so often when both bands at each club were simultaneously on break, we would switch out a couple of musicians in each band. Few in either audience would realize the bait and switch, as most were immersed in heavy drinking and lively dancing.

At our steady gig at the Juke Joint Cafe, which was the same room as the Checker's Theater where I played the musical *Reunion*, we played in a spacious back room to diners in a dinner show format. The owner had it right, using his front room as a separate bar with a band playing happy hour, followed by our show set in the back room. He made sure the band left each night with a take-home meal from the kitchen, in this case some of the best Cajun meals on the planet. Adjacent to the club were artist lofts, four stories high and mostly all rented. The residents began to complain about the noise from the club, eventually mushrooming into a major legal issue that forced the showroom to shut down.

There was a number of different drummers and bass players that came in and out during my three-year stint, including subs for a night, a common scenario in blues bands as most of the chord progressions are the same and the standard tunes are familiar to most, which made it one of the easier gigs to jump on stage for a night without any preparation. Just don't shake hands on stage when you arrive as if you're just meeting the other band members for the first time, although you really are.

Although most nights consisted of the usual grind of cranking out tunes for dancers, we got to play some high-visibility street fairs, the best being Street Scene, a huge annual weekend music fest that featured over 60 bands, some local, but mostly established national acts, past and present, representing all styles on myriad stages. Also, the local Adams Avenue and Encanto Street Fairs showcased us, which was always a great opportunity to play in a concert setting, a welcome reprise from the rigors of predictable nightclub gigs.

Wayne Riker

Band #44: Coupe De Ville

Wayne Riker. Photo: Steve Covault.

One night, in July 1999, while playing with Shelle at a dive bar called Buster Daly's (now U-31) in the North Park neighborhood of San Diego, a local bass player approached me about playing with his band at a bar in Chula Vista called the Manhattan, a long-standing dive bar in the South Bay. I accepted because it was an off weekend from Shelle's band. I asked him for a set list and perhaps a tape of some of the tunes they did. He said not to worry and to just show up, that it was all strictly simple blues tunes, assuring me that I was overqualified for the gig and that they were looking forward to having me play in their band.

Arriving at the club that night I was soon to realize that the lead singer was also the bandleader and front man, who also played harmonica or, in blues circles, a blues harp. After the first song, which turned into a 15-minute blues jam with a seemingly eternal harp solo, followed by their nod to me to take a long series of solos, I sensed an immediate danger between the clientele and the band. After the same lengthy jam format continued on through

the first set, I knew what was about to happen. Sure enough, the owner approached the bandleader and said, "This is a dancing crowd; they wanna dance and you're not playing anything they can dance to." Realizing the dilemma that the band was in, having no dance-able standard tunes, only non-dance-able slow blues tempos, I said, "Give me the mic for the next set and follow me." The bass player and drummer obliged and I set my decades of pro experience in motion, hitting the mic right away with: "Okay folks, let's get up and dance," breaking into Chuck Berry's "Roll Over Beethoven," followed by dance floor favorites, "Ol' Time Rock 'n' Roll," "Brown Eyed Girl," "Proud Mary," "Kansas City," etc.

The night was saved as I led the band the rest of the night, and all went home happy with the club owner thanking me for keeping her customers there drinking and dancing. The band also thanked me and we parted ways after loading out. I never saw any of them again, and they never called me back, as I'm sure they found the appropriate listening rooms to play other than a neighborhood bar with a dance floor, where people just want to drown their sorrows and dance the night away.

Band #45: The Satin Love Orchestra

It was the year 2000, a new century with new technology emerging. Suddenly electronic mail was slowly replacing faxes and phone calls. A bandleader in Eugene, Oregon, contacted me; he had found me on a local music web page, the new Yellow Pages, under the heading "guitar instruction." He read my bio and called me to see if I would be available to play guitar in his eight-piece retro funk band at a Christmas party at the Hotel Del Coronado, the historic landmark right in San Diego's backyard. The date of the holiday gala was December 16th, in the grand ballroom, overlooking the Pacific Ocean and the white sands of Coronado Beach.

The Satin Love Orchestra. Photo: David Putzier.

I had a little less than two weeks to learn their song list, 60 songs total. Most of them involved arrangements from the songbooks of Earth, Wind & Fire, the Ohio Players, Kool & the Gang, the Bee Gees, Herbie Hancock, etc. Luckily I had played about half their list in previous bands, mostly when many of their selected songs were current, so a bit of a refresher course on some of the tunes was all I needed. The unfamiliar half of their list required purchasing the CDs or singles, back in the dark ages before YouTube.

The bandleader mentioned that the guitar player I was replacing was somewhat of a heavy metal-style player, adding that his rhythmic and solo

Wayne Riker

approach to the traditional funk repertoire added a quirky, out-of-the box groove that the bandleader liked. However, he told me to just be myself and play the tunes as written. I spent six hours a day drilling all the rhythmic parts, chords, riffs, and even many of the horn lines and piano parts into my memory bank. As usual, I prepared myself as best I could in a short amount of time.

The band arrived from Oregon that night, consisting of three horns, piano, bass, drums, and a female vocalist, complete with groovy 1970s loud disco garb. The band was tight with high-level musicianship. I had a blast

The Hotel Del Coronado, Coronado, California

playing with them and was proud of the job I did in such a short time frame. The audience would never have known that I was a fill in, and you certainly would never tell them that.

The members of the band all thanked me for the conscientious job I did in learning their tunes, but wouldn't you know, the bandleader pulled me aside and said, "Good job, but I missed not having my regular guitarist; you should hear the way he rips fast metal riffs over these tunes." I didn't even react to it, knowing that the comment reflected the fact that I did too good a job in nailing all the signature riffs and rhythms. Somewhere in his inner world of insecurities, he found it necessary to bring the positive moment down a notch. Little did he know that this was far from my first rodeo, since I was by now a war-tested, grizzled veteran that had been through most every high-stress and challenging gig scenario there is. A few weeks later he sent me a nice note, via the new electronic mail system, thanking me for filling in, which helped them preserve a high paying out of town job.

Band #46: The John Juliano Quartet

Wayne Riker. Photo: Steve Covault.

A fellow local guitarist contacted me in December 2002, inquiring if I could fill in for him at his regular gig at the Ritz Carlton Hotel in Laguna Beach, Orange County, just north of San Diego. It didn't take me long to mull that offer over. Sure, an iconic five-star hotel draped over a scenic cliff overlooking the Pacific Ocean; yep, I'm there. Upon my arrival John, the leader and keyboardist, handed me a large binder with hundreds of tunes charted out, all numbered by title and page, containing a hodgepodge of standards, ranging from jazz to country and rock to Latin.

Although playing top-echelon lounges, especially with ongoing dining, can be an easy, low-stress gig; you often find yourself uninspired, a bit bored, and occasionally nodding off at such gigs that are often called "wallpaper" gigs in the business, where your band might as well be piped-in music, not that I miss the chaotic low-brow bars with drunks falling into your P.A. speakers on the dance floor or yelling out obnoxious song requests. The cushy three-set night was nicely augmented with free range of the staff dining facility, complete with a TV set and microwave. Yeah, high living for lowly musicians.

The Ritz Carlton, Laguna Beach, California

I wound up getting rehired a few more times throughout 2003, each time with a different female vocalist added to the trio. Each one had their own book of musical charts for their songs, which is an asset, as each singer often sings standard tunes in a different key other than the written key, making it easier for the band in not having to transpose the music on the spot.

On my last gig there in 2003, the drummer in the group was the appointed bandleader. After our first break we were all eating in the staff dining room when he summoned us to head back to the stage. I quickly got up and headed out first in order to check my tuning. After we all got on stage, the drummer came over to me and said, "The proper protocol is for me as bandleader to lead the way to the stage with the rest of you in line behind me." Not that it was a big deal, but even me, the quintessential pro who was always doing everything the right way, was quite taken back by how silly and petty that was, but like the old saying goes, "just when you think you've seen everything, something new happens."

Band #47: The Electrocarpathians

The Electrocarpathians: Wayne Riker (third from right), 2004

Bassist Jeff Pekarek and I go back to the early 1980s when we met through mutual musicians. We played a few private parties together as a duo, mostly background music, or, as mentioned, wallpaper gigs. He had been the youngest bassist to play in the San Diego Symphony and a marvelous multi instrumentalist that I like to categorize as a real musician, classically trained and able to sight-read anything.

His long running group, the Electrocarpathians, performs a unique blend of Eastern European folk music, comprised of a band of equally erudite musicians, playing a variety of different string and woodwind instruments. In 2000, I got a call to sub for the guitarist in the group, mind you a daunting task being that many of the charts were in 7/4, 9/8, and 5/4 time. I have a hard enough time reading in 4/4 time, which is one reason I'm usually the last call guitarist on this gig. However, he liked the way I improvised over most of their tunes. At this point in the game, I had learned every which way to tap dance and get by in most all musical situations, charts or no charts.

On May 6, 2000, we arrived to play a wedding reception, only to discover upon our entrance that both the bride's parents had died in the previous month before the wedding. Therefore, the wedding was postponed and the gig turned into a memorial gathering, which changed the requested Eastern European songs for the celebration to playing innocuous instrumental pop tunes as a backdrop for the somber gathering.

March 14, 2004. It was the annual international bash for the Outback

Steakhouse chain. They rented out the entire downtown San Diego Hyatt Islandia Hotel, totaling more than 3,000 in attendance at their convention. Our group, all dressed as gypsies, was expanded to a dozen players, adding in an accordion player, second guitarist, and clarinetist. We split up into three groups of four to cover different rooms of party revelers. It was a symbolic night, as it turned out that a colorful gypsy bandana would be the last of the many hats that I would wear in my lengthy band history.

Wayne Riker. Photo: Steve Covault.

50 Years • 50 Bands • 50 Bucks

Band #48: The Steph Johnson Group

Steph Johnson and Wayne Riker, 2012

On July 23, 2003, I fulfilled a promise to a young singer that I would accompany her to an open mic at a beer joint in the Mission Beach section of San Diego, across from the roar of an old wooden roller coaster and mere footsteps from the Pacific Ocean, appropriately called the Coaster Saloon. A week earlier a guitar student of mine brought Steph Johnson into my teaching studio to get an evaluation of her singing ability. After hearing her sing three songs, I recognized the potential, but recommended she get experience by putting herself out into the scene and meeting other musicians. Her journey began at that open mic night, where we performed the same three tunes she sang for me in my studio: "Heard It Through the Grapevine," "Proud Mary," and "Summertime." She hasn't looked back since.

Flash forward five years to 2008 and we reconnect at a Christmas party, where at this point she's already met and played with half of San Diego, led a few bands of her own, recorded a CD, and had taken up guitar as well. In my case, I was in a reinvention period as a solo acoustic instrumentalist. I invited her to join me as part of a house concert in 2009, and we played three songs together again, but this time they were three of her original tunes, composed on her shiny red Gibson guitar and soon to be appearing on her second CD. It was an attentive audience of 75 folks that heard our performance that night, but it was lost forever when the kid I had videotaping the show forgot to hit the record button.

A few years later in 2011, as I was tutoring her on guitar briefly, she graciously invited me to play

The Coaster Saloon

with her, this time with her sharing lead guitar duties with me. It was at Ki's Restaurant, Ki being one of my former guitar students back in early 1980s, a cozy two-story edifice in Cardiff, overlooking the shores of the Pacific Ocean. We played some jazz standards, Santana tunes, and some of Steph's originals. By now her singing had matured by leaps and bounds and currently the sky is the limit with her guitar and voice melding together as one.

Band #49: SaVi

SaVi: Calexico, California, Wayne Riker (third from left), 2014. Photo: Cynthia Morales.

Between 2005 and 2013 I concentrated on writing original compositions for solo acoustic guitar, recording and performing them in addition to recording full band CDs of original compositions as well. I played a sparse amount of band gigs in that time period. Keyboardist Fred Lanuza played on two of those recordings. We established a close friendship since our bygone days in musical theater, so when he asked if I would play a full band gig with his seven-piece Latin band, I was glad to oblige despite the fact that the gig date was also on my 64th birthday, November 24, 2014.

After a three-hour rehearsal it felt good to get back in the saddle on electric guitar, playing some hip progressive jazz tunes and Fred's original compositions. The gig was at the San Diego State campus in Calexico, California, a border town a stone's throw from Mexico. I left on the two-hour drive from San Diego in plenty of time to spare, knowing always to allow myself extra time in case of car trouble or such.

Arriving in Calexico with a few hours to spare, I was cruising around in search of a place to eat when I suddenly realized that I was on a short one-way street a few hundred feet from the entry gate to Mexico. Greeted by the machine gun-yielding guards, I asked if I could turn around. They said I could after I entered Mexico, adding that there would be a u-turn a mile south. They were right, except now I was stuck in a bumper-to-bumper wait of an hour or so to re-enter the U.S. I called Fred to explain my predicament and that I should be there on time regardless.

Finally reaching the U.S. entry, I felt relieved, only to discover that my only form of ID was my driver's license. I explained my situation that I accidentally drove across the border, in which the border agent replied, "A driver's license just tells me you can drive a car. You need a birth certificate, passport, or ID card from the Post Office." He then slipped back into his booth and seemed to be checking my life's history on his computer.

Wayne Riker in 2015, McGee's Tavern, Fallbrook, California. Photo: Kenneth Ray Seals.

All seemed good until another border agent was approaching my car with two mean-looking German Shepherds. I should have known. Long hair, musician, and no proper ID; they must have thought I was a drug smuggler. By now I had been detained for 20 minutes, when I thought of a way to prove my innocence. I opened my trunk and showed them my guitar and amp, along with an appointment book that contained the details and directions to the campus. That seemed to satisfy them. The one agent then proceeded to hand me a pamphlet on traveling in Mexico, including the rules and regulations of entering the country.

I still arrived at the gig on time, with my travails making for a good conversation piece while loading into the campus auditorium. The gig was fantastic—great musicians and a full house of appreciative music aficionados. The pay was good too, although it was a "check's in the mail" gig, which usually meant payment would be received within anywhere from two weeks to two months. Curiously, the next day my cell phone company informed me of a $19.99 charge I had incurred the previous day. After pondering the charge for a few minutes, it dawned on me, "Oh yeah, the call to Fred from the u-turn back to the U.S. was an international phone call. Oh well, happy birthday!

Band #50: Celeste Lanuza Band

The Celeste Lanuza Band: Wayne Riker (far right) 2015

My kids and Fred Lanuza's kids were mere toddlers when Fred and I started working together, in 1989, at the San Diego Rep for the musical *Are You Lonesome Tonight?* Again, in lieu of our friendship, I was glad to join forces in a backup band for his now 25-year-old rising pop star daughter, Celeste.

She had just released a CD with original tunes, written by herself and her dad, and was invited to showcase her talents at the House of Blues in downtown San Diego on March 18, 2015. The ten-piece band, backup singers included, was a solid group of A-list players.

We had two lengthy rehearsals before the show, both at 10 a.m., which in musician's time is equivalent to 6 a.m. The set list was a challenging group of pop, Latin, and jazz charts with full-on out-front vocals, a great repertoire for what would be my final band hurrah. Even though Fred wanted to make this project a permanent band, I knew my days of full-time bands would be in the rear view mirror after this gig, My cup was full after all the many twists and turns over a half century's time since I first pushed down on a fret and heard a clear sounding note.

There were a few acts before we went on as the headliner. It was a great sounding room with an engaging audience cheering us on. Nothing like hav-

House of Blues, San Diego, 2015. Photo: Traci Smith.

ing a great house system with two competent dudes running sound while playing a compact one-hour show set. That's the way it should be in the end—a concert setting with a cooking band, fully at peace with my round trip around the game board of bands with no regrets!

Epilogue

Since these memoirs focused on 50 years playing guitar with 50 subsequent vignettes, and yes many of the gigs in and around 50 bucks earned, I omitted details of concurrent career landmarks as a teacher, author, instructional columnist, and recording artist.

I taught private guitar lessons from 1973 until 2014 in New York City; Topeka, Kansas; Rochester, Minnesota; and San Diego, California, with student loads as low as four students a week to as high as 65 students a week, in whatever style a student wanted to learn. My proudest achievement, other than offering encouragement and inspiration to all that entered my teaching quarters, was that I never missed teaching a lesson due to illness, I never called in sick.

I also taught privately at Frances Parker Lower School in San Diego for two years, in 1991 and 1992, and taught a group class at Coleman Tech High in San Diego, two separate classes, five days a week during the school year, in 2012-2013.

Between 1990 and 2006, I was a senior faculty member for the National Guitar Workshop, a music camp and workshop held at eight different select campuses around the U.S. during the summer months, teaching mainly electric blues classes as well as a similar role with Guitar Workshop Plus in 2015 and 2016.

Between 1994 and 2006, I authored eight blues guitar instructional books with Alfred Publishing, distributed worldwide with appropriate language translations.

Wayne Riker with Guitar Workshop Plus Blues class, Cal State San Marcos, 2015

Between 1989 and 2012, I intermittently produced instructional columns for some of the trade magazines, including *Acoustic Musician*, *Guitar Player*, *Premier Guitar*, and *Acoustic Guitar* magazines.

Between 2008 and 2015, I recorded nine CDs under my own name, three solo guitar recordings, and six with full bands. Seven of the nine CDs contain all original instrumental compositions; the other two CDs are all cover tunes.

When I decided to turn my hobby into a profession, I made a bucket list of five goals I wanted to accomplish along the way: 1) Avoid a "real" job at all costs, other than teaching guitar and playing gigs. 2) Play on a cruise ship. 3) Author guitar instructional books. 4) Write instructional columns for *Guitar Player* magazine. 5) Compose and record my original instrumental tunes. Mission accomplished!

This unlikely musical journey was lots of hard work, based on the

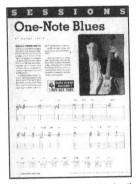

Guitar Player magazine, April 1998 issue

Thomas Edison ingredient for success: "99% perspiration, 1% inspiration." In order to persevere, these were my survive-and-advance mantras: 1) Accept every challenge with no fear, confidence, and excitement. 2) Accept every disappointment with renewed vigor and hope for a positive outcome the next time. All roads to success are littered with failure. 3) Listen and learn from constructive criticism. 4) Respect the music you're playing, whether it's your cup of tea or not. 5) Learn as many styles as you can; it can lead to a wider range of employment. 6) Learn the basic standard tunes in each style. 7) Know your chords inside and out; playing them correctly will at least get you in the door. 8) Be prepared when you come to rehearsals; have your parts down and ready to go. 9) Don't be late for anything. 10) Strong social skills is a plus. 11) Don't whine or complain, do your job; rehearsals or band meetings are the best times to present issues. 12) Be courteous and polite to those around you.

All these factors helped me have an advantage over many other musicians who fell by the wayside because they didn't adhere to some of these common-sense factors. Notice that some are musical factors and some are simple common-sense principles. Playing music is a true high, but it's also a business.

Finally, speaking of high, I never partook in the drug scene as I wanted to reach my goals with a clear state of mind, although a friend in high school turned me on to smoking pipe tobacco, a habit that festered for 30 years on and off until I quit in 1998. It did help calm me during my excessive practice regimens, and it was a vice of choice that helped me stay away from all other substances.

There is one vice, however. I started at the beginning of my musical journey, which has remained as a constant throughout. Drum roll

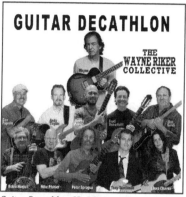

Guitar Decathlon CD, 2012

please: two cups of coffee a day, starting at Callahan's in Fort Lee, New Jersey, and continuing a half century later at my

local Starbucks in Solana Beach, California. And on that note, cheers and best of luck in your journey in life, whatever that may be.

Wayne Riker. Photo: Steve Covault.

Website:

www.waynerikerguitar.com

Work hard
in silence
let success
make the noise

Made in the USA
San Bernardino, CA
08 July 2016